Frank Parkin was educated at the London School of
Economics. He teaches sociology at the University of Kent
at Canterbury and is working on a comparative study of
socialist societies. He is the author of *Middle Class
Radicalism*.

Frank Parkin

Class Inequality and Political Order

Social Stratification in Capitalist and Communist Societies

Paladin

Granada Publishing Limited
Published in 1972 by Paladin
Frogmore, St Albans, Herts AL2 2NF
Reprinted 1973, 1975 (twice)

First published by MacGibbon & Kee Ltd 1971
Copyright © Frank Parkin 1971
Made and printed in Great Britain by
Richard Clay (The Chaucer Press) Ltd
Bungay, Suffolk
Set in Monotype Ehrhardt

For Dinah and Charley

Contents

Preface

I started this book with the vague intention of writing a general
introduction to social stratification. This threatened to contain
all the standard set-pieces on estates, caste, class, race, and the
like, which fill out the fat American textbooks on sociology. It
was not really until I came face-to-face with this prospect that I
fully appreciated how dull such books must be to read; they
must be even duller to write. The approach I adopted instead
was to write about only those issues which interested me and to
forget the rest. This means that I have confined my attention to
a few key problems of stratification and inequality in modern
capitalist and socialist societies. The end product is thus not so
much a consecutive narrative as a series of chapters on a set of
closely connected themes. Perhaps the main unifying strand
running through the book is to be found in my treatment of the
relationship between dominant and subordinate classes. My
underlying assumption throughout is that this relationship is
essentially an exploitative one and as such confronts the dominant class with serious problems of social control. Hence the
title of the book. The plan of approach is as follows.

In Chapter 1 I discuss the process of class formation in a
market system and the related issue of the distribution of social
honour. Much of the discussion here is devoted to a critique of
currently fashionable neo-Weberian approaches to stratification.
In particular, certain doubts are cast upon the validity of 'multi-
dimensional' models of the reward structure. I suggest that
Weber's key propositions relating to class and status have been
somewhat trivialized by his present-day followers; and that their
heavy emphasis on the subjective components of stratification

has encouraged a misunderstanding of the link between factual and normative aspects of class inequality.

Chapter 2 examines some of the more important social mechanisms which have what might be called a 'safety-valve' effect on the system of inequalities. Of particular relevance here is the process of social mobility and its impact on the political order. Also considered is the role of socialization agencies in tailoring men's expectations to the realities of the opportunity structure. Chapter 3 explores systematic variations in the social interpretations given to inequality. I suggest it is useful to distinguish three major 'meaning-systems', each of which promotes a different response to the facts of inequality. These I call the 'dominant', 'subordinate', and 'radical' meaning-systems. The first derives from the dominant institutional orders of society, and presents what might be called the 'official' version of social inequality. The second derives from the working-class community setting, and promotes various modes of adjustment or accommodation to subordinate status. The third has its source in the mass political party of the subordinate class and presents an oppositional view of the reward system. I argue that most members of the subordinate class are exposed, in varying degrees, to all three of these meaning-systems, and that this affects their overall perceptions of political and social reality. Finally in this chapter a question mark is put against the continuation of radical perceptions in Britain and other countries where the mass working-class party has virtually ceased to disseminate an oppositional view of the reward system.

Chapters 4 and 5 pursue this theme of the relationship between mass working-class parties and the stratification order. Chapter 4 discusses the impact made by Social Democratic or Labour governments upon the balance of class advantages in capitalist societies. This is done by comparing aspects of class inequality in European societies which have had majority Labour governments in modern times (notably Britain and the Scandinavian countries) and those which have not. This is followed by a brief discussion of the social factors which have encouraged the long-term de-radicalization of Social Democracy. Chapter 5 continues in similar vein by examining the reward structure of European societies in which the Communist

Party occupies the seat of power. One of the problems considered here is whether, or in what sense, European socialist states could be said to be class stratified along the same lines as their capitalist neighbours. The main propositions arising from this debate are briefly assessed in the light of available evidence, in particular that relating to the emergence of a 'new class' of white-collar professionals and party bureaucrats. This discussion spills over into Chapter 6, which suggests a number of important contrasts between capitalist and socialist systems of inequality and the tensions they give rise to.

It will be apparent that these are all large and complex issues; they certainly deserve much more extended treatment than I have been able to give them here. My plea is that I have more often attempted to pose questions than to provide answers. At the same time, though, I have tried not to be ultra-cautious or to avoid stating anything resembling a definite point of view. On the contrary, many arguments are framed in such a way as to put my neck squarely on the chopping block. I am sure there will be no shortage of potential executioners.

My colleagues at the University of Kent have been more than generous in their help, criticism, and advice. To name them all would read too much like a Faculty roll-call.

University of Kent,   FRANK PARKIN
Canterbury, February 1970

1   The Dimensions of Class Inequality

Inequalities associated with the class system are founded upon two interlocking, but conceptually distinct, social processes. One is the allocation of rewards attaching to different *positions* in the social system; the other is the process of *recruitment* to these positions. Modern societies do of course exhibit both forms of inequality, but social theorists and political reformers have tended to distinguish between them and to evaluate them somewhat differently. Thus, the egalitarian critique of the class system raises objections to the wide disparities of reward accruing to different positions. On what grounds, it is asked, is it morally legitimate to give greater economic and social benefits to one set of occupations than to another, when each in its own way contributes to the social good? Generally, egalitarians have espoused a view of social justice which asks that men be rewarded in accordance with their individual social needs, family responsibilities, and the like, rather than in accordance with their role in the division of labour. The meritocratic critique of the class system, on the other hand, is less concerned about inequalities of reward accruing to different positions than about the process of recruitment to these positions. The prime objection raised is against present restrictions on the opportunities for talented but lowly born people to improve their personal lot. Seen from this angle, social justice entails not so much the equalization of rewards as the equalization of opportunities to compete for the most privileged positions.

Although the processes of rewarding and recruitment are analytically separable they are closely intertwined in the actual operation of the stratification system. This is to a large extent to do with the prominent part played by the family in 'placing' individuals at various points in the class hierarchy. There is a marked tendency for those who occupy relatively privileged positions to ensure that their own progeny are recruited into similar positions. The ability of well-placed families to confer advantages on their younger members thus encourages a fairly high degree of social self-recruitment within privileged strata from one generation to the next. Partly as a result of this there often develops a pattern of social and cultural differentiation which, in turn, reinforces the system of occupational recruitment and so crystallizes the class structure through time. It is this interplay between material and normative or cultural aspects of inequality which gives rise to class stratification. For stratification implies not simply inequality, but a set of institutional arrangements which guarantee a fairly high degree of *social continuity* in the reward position of family units through the generations. Without the long-term continuity provided by the kinship link it would still be possible for inequality to persist, but not class stratification in the conventional meaning of that term.

The failure of some writers to recognize that the family, not the individual, is the appropriate social unit of the class system has led to certain confusions in their analysis. Not infrequently, collectivities of individuals having particular attributes in common, such as age or sex, are designated as units of stratification. Women, for example, by virtue of the disabilities they suffer in comparison with men, or the young, by virtue of the disabilities they suffer in comparison with adults, are sometimes regarded as social units comparable to a subordinate class or racial minority. Lenski is one of the main proponents of this view, arguing that what he calls 'class systems' based on age and sex are to be regarded as important dimensions of stratification in modern society.[1]

Now female status certainly carries many disadvantages compared with that of males in various areas of social life including employment opportunities, property ownership, income, and so on. However, these inequalities associated with sex differences are not usefully thought of as components of stratification. This is because for the great majority of women the allocation of social and economic rewards is determined primarily by the position of their families – and, in particular, that of the male head. Although women today share certain status attributes in common, simply by virtue of their sex, their claims over resources are not primarily determined by their own occupation but, more commonly, by that of their fathers or husbands. And if the wives and daughters of unskilled labourers have some things in common with the wives and daughters of wealthy landowners, there can be no doubt that the *differences* in their overall situation are far more striking and significant. Only if the disabilities attaching to female status were felt to be so great as to override differences of a class kind would it be realistic to regard sex as an important dimension of stratification. But in modern society the 'vertical' placement of women in the class hierarchy, through membership of a kin group, appears to be much more salient to female self-perception and identity than the status of womanhood *per se*. It is perhaps for this reason that feminist political movements appear to have had relatively little appeal for the majority of women. Because the major unit of reward is the family, wives and daughters do not generally feel their interests to be in opposition to those of their male kin. Inequalities between different members of the family thus cannot really be said to provide the basis for a distinct form of social stratification.

It is on similar grounds that we must reject the argument that youth represents a class or stratum with interests of its own in opposition to those of adults. Again, it can readily be accepted that the young do suffer certain material and social disadvantages in comparison with their seniors. Rates of pay for the young are almost always below those commanded by older men, even where the tasks performed are not noticeably different. In addition, young people in employment contribute proportionately more to welfare payments in relation to the demands they make on health and similar services. In time of war, the sacrifices required of young males in the defence of adult institutions are especially high. Again, the legal status of adolescents is often a disadvantaged one; there are numerous prohibitions concerning such matters as property ownership, marriage, drinking, driving vehicles, and the like. Similarly, in their day-to-day lives the young are continuously exposed to adult authority and domination, and very few areas of personal autonomy and independence are available to them. This combination of factors has led to the suggestion that modern youth shares a similar class position, with all the political implications that this potentially entails. As Lenski sees it:

Of all the class struggles in modern societies, the most underrated may prove to be those between *age classes*, especially those between youth (in the sense of adolescents and young adults) and adults. The importance of this struggle is so underestimated, in fact, that its existence is typically overlooked altogether in discussion of class struggles, or confused with economic class struggles. Nevertheless, there is considerable evidence to indicate that the struggle between age classes is a distinctive class struggle in its own right and, furthermore, is one of the more serious and least tractable.[2]

Lenski concludes that, '. . . ideal conditions for class conflict, as identified by Marx, have been created . . . The net result is that struggles between the generations . . . are likely to take violent and even revolutionary forms.'[3] John and Margaret Reynolds have similarly argued that, under conditions of advanced capitalism, 'The young . . . form the new proletariat, are undergoing impoverishment, and can become the new revolutionary class.'[4] These views are not particularly convincing. In the first place, adolescence or youth is a temporary and transitional status; the disadvantages that accrue specifically to the young have been borne by every member of society, and must be suffered for a relatively short time. Because every adolescent expects to become an adult there is none of that sense of being permanently trapped in an inferior social status which has characterized the fate of so many other under-privileged groups. Again, the life chances of the young are by no means standardized, but differ sharply according to parental status. Such similarities as there are in the overall position of the young hold for the very short run only. And in so far as adolescence is also a period of social preparation for recruitment to adult positions, it could easily be argued that the similarities in the life experiences of young people in different classes are more apparent than real.

The tendency to define attributes such as age and sex as elements of stratification is generally associated with the conceptual presentation of stratification as a 'multi-dimensional' phenomenon. According to the *International Encyclopedia of the Social Sciences*, 'It is fundamental that social stratification is multi-dimensional.' Furthermore, sociologists who question this basic assumption tend to do so because, 'for ideological reasons they want the term "class" to refer to some single, simple and all-explanatory notion'.[5] In this view, there is no one dominant source of inequality in modern society, but many different sources, each independent of and cross-cutting the other to produce a complex patchwork of rewards and privileges. The stratification order is seen to comprise a variety of distinct 'rank dimensions', such as occupation, ethnic status, education, income, religion, sex, age, and so on. Each individual occupies a certain rank on each of these different dimensions, rather than a single position in the reward structure. To be high on one particular dimension is not necessarily to be high on any other; indeed, a great deal of inconsistency between ranks is commonly found, so that any individual's total sum of material and social benefits may be made up of quite variable increments. This 'multi-dimensional' view of the reward system is perhaps useful in analysing societies like the United States which are highly differentiated in terms of race or ethnicity, religious affiliations, and sharp regional variations (especially between north and south) as well as by social classes. But in societies like Britain, and many other European countries, multiple cleavages of this kind tend to be rather less marked, so that the multi-dimensional model would seem to be less applicable. Even as far as the United States is concerned, such an approach is difficult to reconcile with the notion of stratification as a system of structured inequality. To plot each person's position on a variety of different dimensions tends to produce statistical categories composed of those who have a similar 'status profile'; but it does not identify the type of *social collectivities* or *classes* which have traditionally been the subject matter of stratification. Such an approach tends to obscure the systematic nature of inequality and the fact that it is grounded in the material order in a fairly identifiable fashion.

The origins of the multi-dimensional approach are to be found in Weber's writings on stratification. Weber suggested that societies were stratified along various non-material as well as material lines, and that although the different forms of inequality tended to correspond, certain systematic discrepancies between them did occur. It was pointed out, for example, that in nineteenth-century Europe the industrial and mercantile *nouveaux riches* occupied high material status, but in terms of social honour they ranked below the aristocracy, the members of which were often less well off economically. This disjunction between class and status positions could not be apprehended by the Marxist model of stratification, since this drew no important distinction between material and symbolic aspects of inequality. Weber's approach thus resulted in a refinement of Marx's model although, as we shall later see, the kinds of discrepancies he was able to point up do not always quite apply to the conditions of modern industrialism. Weber's present day followers are often insufficiently cautious in applying certain of his key concepts to the analysis of contemporary Western societies. Whereas Weber followed Marx in making classes or strata the main focus of concern, there has been a tendency among neo-Weberians to conceive of the stratification order as highly fragmented and reducible to a patchwork of statistical aggregates. In some respects, the multi-dimensional approach has led to the trivialization of Weber's ideas, in particular through exaggerated claims regarding the functional independence of different aspects of inequality such as class and status. This is an issue we consider later in this chapter, when we come to examine the distribution of social honour. But first it is necessary to turn to the process of class formation.

2

The backbone of the class structure, and indeed of the entire reward system of modern Western society, is the occupational order. Other sources of economic and symbolic advantage do coexist alongside the occupational order, but for the vast majority of the population these tend, at best, to be secondary to those deriving from the division of labour. As Blau and Duncan express it:

The occupational structure in modern industrial society not only constitutes an important foundation for the main dimensions of social stratification but also serves as the connecting link between different institutions and spheres of social life, and therein lies its great significance. The hierarchy of prestige strata and the hierarchy of economic classes have their roots in the occupational structure; so does the hierarchy of political power and authority, for political authority in modern society is largely exercised as a full time occupation . . . The occupational structure also is the link between the economy and the family, through which the economy affects the family's status and the family supplies manpower to the economy.[6]

As far as advanced Western capitalist societies are concerned, we can represent the backbone of the reward system as a hierarchy of broad occupational categories. This runs from high to low as follows:

Professional, managerial, and administrative.
Semi-professional and lower administrative.
Routine white-collar.
Skilled manual.
Semi-skilled manual.
Unskilled manual.

Although sociologists seem generally agreed that this represents a rough profile of the reward hierarchy, there is much less agreement as to why the distribution of social and material benefits flows along these lines. In the view of some writers, inequalities of reward are to be explained in terms of differences in the functional importance of various positions. That is, occupations which are most crucial to the maintenance of the social order tend to be accorded greater rewards than occupations which make less contribution to this end. As many critics have pointed out, however, the claim that positions can be scaled in terms of their functional importance is a highly doubtful one; to suggest, for example, that managers are more highly rewarded than factory workers because they make a greater contribution to the productive system is to offer more of a value judgement than an explanation. Other writers, in opposition to the functionalist view, have suggested that what ultimately determines the distribution of rewards and of structured inequality generally, is power. Thus, in a recent statement, Dahrendorf has advanced the proposition that 'the system of inequality that we call social stratification is only a secondary consequence of the social structure of power'.[7] In similar vein, Lenski has argued that 'The distribution of rewards in a society is a function of the distribution of power, not of system needs.'[8]

To introduce the notion of power into explanations of inequality is a useful corrective to the functionalist view; but it is an approach which raises obvious problems of its own. For example, it would be true in a sense to claim that managerial and professional personnel receive higher rewards than manual labourers because they are more powerful, and not because they are more important to society. But the question which this immediately raises is, what makes them more powerful? We cannot take inequalities of power as somehow given and unproblematic; we have to specify what it is that accounts for variations in men's ability to stake successful claims to rewards. In the context of the occupational order of modern capitalist society this ultimately boils down to specifying the conditions which make for success in the market-place. Curiously enough, in their attempts to account for the distribution of rewards, sociologists have tended to pay scant attention to the role of the market – certainly in comparison with the work of economists. This is partly because sociological generalizations have usually sought to encompass all or most forms of structured inequality, whether in feudal, peasant, caste, or industrial societies. As a result, theories have been pitched at a fairly high level of abstraction, with consequent neglect of the distributive mechanisms which may be unique to specific types of society. Indeed, the disappointing results of attempts to theorize about stratification in all its forms are perhaps largely due to fundamental differences in the bases of reward in industrial and non-industrial societies. At least so far as modern capitalist societies are concerned, the role of the market in allocating rewards via the occupational order seems crucial to the entire stratification system; so much so that the search for uniformities with other types of society which lack an industrial occupational structure is almost bound to be unilluminating. Let us then consider in some detail the relationship between class and market in societies of the modern Western variety.

If we examine the scale of occupational categories set out on page 19 it is apparent that it represents not only an approximate hierarchy of rewards, but also an approximate hierarchy of skills – or at least the kind of skills in demand within an industrial order. Broadly considered, occupational groupings which stand high in the scale of material and symbolic advantages also tend to rank high in the possession of marketable skills; those which are less well rewarded tend to be relatively low in such skills. This correspondence may not necessarily hold for every single occupation, but it is certainly the case for the broad occupational categories now being considered. There is no Western industrial society which allocates greater benefits to unskilled than to skilled occupational categories, or higher benefits to semi-professional than to professional categories. In other words, marketable expertise is the most important single determinant of occupational reward, and therefore one of the key elements in the system of class inequality. Expressed in a somewhat different way, and in fairly general terms, it could be said that the greater the skills or knowledge commanded by an occupation, the greater is its relative scarcity in the market-place. And, in turn, it is the degree of scarcity relative to demand which largely determines occupational reward. Thus, those in professional and managerial positions are allocated a more favourable share of resources than are manual labourers primarily because they command the type of skills whose scarcity-value furnishes them with the power to stake larger claims. To be sure, positions which rank high in expertise generally attempt to maintain or enhance their scarcity, and thus their reward-power, by various institutional means. Doctors, lawyers, academics, and professionals in general, commonly attempt to control the number of new recruits by imposing stiff entrance qualifications and insisting on long and expensive periods of training. By this and similar strategies the sitting incumbents can keep a strict control over numbers, so that scarcity-value may be maintained 'artificially' over time. Comparable techniques are practised by skilled manual occupations, such as printers, where entry is controlled by the insistence on potential members serving lengthy apprenticeships. Although long and often costly training is usually defended as an essential preliminary to skilled or professional work, there is little doubt that much of it is of little practical value, and is simply a device for restricting the supply of labour. The persistent efforts of many white-collar occupations to become professionalized may be understood, in part at least, as an attempt to enhance their market scarcity and so increase their power to claim rewards.

It should be borne in mind that it is no simple matter for an occupation to restrict its supply in this way. For the most part only those occupations which command a fair degree of expertise to begin with are able to improve their market situation still further through control over the supply of new entrants. Unskilled occupations on the whole are not likely to be very successful at creating 'artificial' scarcity for the simple reason that if the tasks they perform are quickly and easily learned the supply of potential labour is relatively plentiful. Rare examples of groups low in skills which have succeeded in controlling entry are dockers and porters in central meat and vegetable markets. These groups tend to draw their members from the immediate neighbourhood in which the industry is situated; and in so far as they form residential as well as work units it may be somewhat easier for them to employ social controls in matters of recruitment. But as far as the great majority of unskilled or low-skilled groups are concerned their unfavourable position in the market-place is not readily offset by techniques of this kind, including trade union organization. If this were not so, if unionization among the unskilled workers could decisively alter their position relative to the skilled groups, then we should not find as we do a broad relationship between skill hierarchy and reward hierarchy which has persisted through time.

There is no need for us to adopt the extreme view that variations in occupational rewards are determined wholly and exclusively by differences in the degree of market power. It can certainly be acknowledged that social influences not related to the market complicate the picture so far presented. For example, traditional ideas about the relative status of certain occupations may play some part in preserving income differentials intact. Again, certain of the non-pecuniary advantages which white-collar groups enjoy over blue-collar groups are more easily explained by reference to societal values than to market rationality. All this is accepted; but the point remains that in a market economy these social or traditional elements are best regarded as secondary rather than primary determinants of occupational reward. Customs and traditions are not usually sufficiently powerful in themselves to run counter to market forces in the long run. This is well illustrated by the relative decline in the rewards of clerical work since the turn of the century, following the spread of literacy and elementary education. As one authority on labour economics has put it:

In sum, differences in pay seem to owe less to the conventional than to the market forces. It may even be that instead of opinions about what is fair having shaped the pay structure, it is the structure that has shaped the opinions. It is to the supply schedules of labour for different jobs that the pay structure seems to owe its main proportions.[9]

It is because we are here concerned with the 'main proportions' of the reward system that our focus is upon occupational categories, and not upon individual occupations. This or that particular occupation may well prove to run counter to the generalization presented above. But when social stratification is the issue under review it is probably just as doubtful, sociologically, to single out the attributes of specific occupations as it is to single out the attributes of specific individuals. Once we take broad occupational categories as our unit of analysis, then the relationship between marketable skills and level of reward stands out quite unambiguously.

3

So far our attention has been focused on the inequalities associated with the division of labour. But in Western capitalist societies an additional source of inequality is that stemming from the ownership of property. Property, and income from property, is far more unevenly distributed than is income from occupation. In Britain, as in other European societies, a relatively tiny minority of the population owns the great bulk of property, including land.[10] Indeed, because property ownership is so heavily concentrated in the hands of so few, it does not figure as the primary source of reward for the mass of the population. The long-run tendency in Western societies has been for the share of national income accruing to property steadily to diminish relative to income from employment.[11] With an ever greater proportion of the adult population drawn into the labour market, the occupational order has come increasingly to set its stamp on the reward structure, despite the persistence of a propertied *élite*. It would in any case seem that the occupational order is now closely associated with property ownership in its more modest forms. This is because those in well-rewarded occupations tend to be able to increase their personal wealth through the investment of surplus earnings. This is a strategy which appears to be common among salaried or professional people, especially in inflationary periods – as witnessed in Britain by the growth of unit trusts appealing to the small investor. Inequalities generated by property may thus be accentuated not only by way of the *inheritance* of great wealth, but much more commonly by way of the *accumulation* of modest wealth on the part of those in well rewarded occupations. Thus to characterize the occupational order as the backbone of the reward structure is not to ignore the role of property, but to acknowledge the interrelationship between the one and the other.

The picture of the reward system which emerges from all this is one marked out by a hierarchy of broad occupational categories each representing a different position in the scale of material and non-material benefits. Although it is possible to demarcate these categories from one another in some approximate fashion, we cannot usefully regard them as each forming a distinct social class. This is partly because the reward hierarchy does not exhibit sharp discontinuities, or cut-off points, between each major occupational grouping. For the most part, the flow of rewards takes the form of a graduated continuum, rather than a series of sharply defined steps. The latter arrangement is much more characteristic of non-industrial stratification systems than of a modern class system. Nevertheless, the fact that we do speak of a class system suggests that we can distinguish some significant 'break' in the reward hierarchy. In Western capitalist societies, this line of cleavage falls between the manual and non-manual occupational categories. The logic behind this claim is that differences in the reward position of white-collar or non-manual groups are less marked than are the similarities, when compared with the situation of blue-collar or manual categories. It should be emphasized that this division does not rest upon mere differences of income; indeed, there is clearly a good deal of overlap in the actual earnings of groups which cluster at the margins of the class-dividing line. But when we speak of rewards, and even more narrowly of material rewards, we mean much more than income. For example, when comparing the position of blue-collar groups with that of white-collar groups, including those in *lower* occupational categories, it is necessary to take account of various concealed or long-term advantages which the latter enjoy over the former. Wedderburn and Craig, in their 1969 study of employment conditions in British industry, have documented these inequalities in some detail.[12] They point out, for example, that in 43 per cent of the establishments investigated, there was no sick pay scheme for manual workers, although well over 90 per cent of clerical and managerial grades were covered by such schemes. Again, one quarter of all firms had no pension schemes for manual workers, whereas almost all had pension coverage for white-collar staff. Further, even where pension schemes were available for both kinds of employee the methods of calculating the pension due were different, tending to favour the managerial and clerical staff. The latter also enjoyed longer paid holidays than did manual workers in more than 60 per cent of establishments. With regard to time keeping, 90 per cent of blue-collar workers were subject to loss of pay for lateness, as against only 8 per cent of clerical employees. The great majority of firms also declared their willingness to pay their white-collar staff during time taken off for domestic reasons; less than a third extended the same privilege to their manual workers.[13] Other differences in the reward position of blue- and white-collar workers have also been established. The latter's advantages include: better promotion and career opportunities; greater long-term economic security and, for many, guaranteed annual salary increases on an incremental scale; a cleaner, less noisy, less dangerous, and generally more comfortable work environment; greater freedom of movement and less supervision, and so forth. All in all, then, even allowing for some overlap in the incomes of blue- and white-collar categories, we are bound to conclude, with Wedderburn and Craig, that 'the big divide still comes between manual workers on the one hand and non-manual grades on the other'. Some differences do of course exist within these two broad classes – between, say, craftsmen and labourers, or between managerial and clerical staff. But because 'manual workers both skilled and unskilled, with the same employer, tend to have fairly *homogeneous* conditions of employment', and because non-manual categories, 'even when they diverge are more like one another than they are like manual workers',[14] we are justified in drawing our class boundary line between the blue-collar and white-collar categories.

It is the highly patterned nature of the inequalities we have so far examined which enables us to portray the reward system in terms of a dichotomous or two-class model. At the same time, to make this translation from broad occupational categories to *class* categories involves us in the consideration of something rather more than the kinds of inequalities discussed above. The concept of class embraces also an array of social and symbolic elements which, although rooted in the material order, take on an existential quality and so in turn react upon this order. To discuss the normative and social components of class is to discuss the nature of the institutional and political arrangements which underlie the distribution of advantages. In broad terms it focuses attention on the social mechanisms by which, within the context of a dichotomous class model, the dominant class seeks to preserve its rewards and privileges *vis-à-vis* the subordinate class. Class conflict may thus be said to reside in the attempt to gain access to, or control over, those institutions which govern the distribution of symbolic and material advantages. These include not only formal political and governmental bodies, but also those associated with the educational system, the productive system, the major socializing agencies, and indeed the whole complex of administrative, judicial, and law-enforcement agencies that we commonly call the 'state'. The state should not be thought of as a clearly bounded institution separate from and independent of the industrial, legal, educational, and political sectors of society; it is more usefully thought of as the institutional embodiment of all these sectors. In so far as it has a distinct function and responsibility it is the mobilization and use, or potential use, of collective force in the defence of existing institutions. And in so far as existing institutional arrangements generally tend to favour the dominant rather than the subordinate class, the relationship between the state and the overall stratification system seems clear enough. Sociologically, the state could be defined as an institutional complex which is the political embodiment of the values and interests of the dominant class. That is to say, the ability of the dominant class to maintain a privileged position for themselves and their progeny rests largely on the fact that representatives of this class have greater access to or control over the various agencies which govern the allocation of rewards than have members or representatives of the subordinate class. The state plays an important role in preserving the structure of class inequality by giving powerful institutional and legal backing to the rules and procedures which decide the distribution of advantages and the process of recruitment to different positions. In modern capitalist society, for example, the educational system, and the legal and social arrangements which protect private property and the operation of market forces, are highly instrumental in buttressing existing inequalities and the privileges of the dominant class through time. As we have seen, the market plays a key part in determining occupational rewards in our type of society. By rewarding positions on the basis of their scarcity value, as settled by the 'laws' of supply and demand, occupations with command over skills and expertise are more advantaged than those lacking such attributes. The fact that market principles, rather than some *other* set of criteria, are legitimized as the main determinants of reward is not, of course, unrelated to the fact that dominant class occupations are themselves well placed in the market. If the criterion of occupational reward was, say, the degree of physical effort involved in the work, or its dirtiness or danger, then professional and white-collar positions would be relatively disadvantaged, compared with most blue-collar positions. Thus by giving legal and institutional backing to the 'laws' of supply and demand, the

27

state effectively buttresses existing inequalities of reward in favour of the non-manual or dominant class. If the state were to fail to use its powers in support of market principles, and were to admit a set of counter-principles as the primary determinant of reward, then the privileged position of the dominant class would be seriously at risk. However, it seems likely that this could only occur if representatives of the dominant class lost control of the key institutions which comprise the state. At any rate, it is doubtful if a dominant class in any society would voluntarily jettison the distributive system upon which its own privileges were founded.

4

Let us now shift our attention from the material or class aspects of the stratification order to certain of its symbolic aspects. We need in particular to consider the allocation of social honour or social status, since this too is commonly regarded as a valuable and unevenly distributed resource. The immediate issue which confronts us here is the relationship between class inequality on the one hand and status inequality on the other. In the view of many sociologists, class and status are to be regarded as functionally distinct and separate dimensions of stratification. The claim is that although the distribution of honour often corresponds fairly closely to the distribution of material reward, the two are not always in conjunction and, in fact, often display considerable inconsistency. In other words, status cannot be treated simply as a symbolic expression of the class structure since it is to some extent generated independently of that structure. In Max Weber's words, 'status honor need not necessarily be linked with a class situation. On the contrary, it normally stands in sharp opposition to the pretensions of sheer property.'[15] This contrast between the two forms of stratification is elaborated in his subsequent remarks that in periods of economic stress class conflicts typically come to the fore, whereas in times of economic stability status concerns tend to predominate. Weber's discussion of social honour, or its more popular synonyms, status and prestige, is generally understood as a successful attempt to replace – or at least improve upon – Marx's model of stratification. By taking account of subjective factors, the cleavages generated by the economic order could be shown to have less significance than Marx invested them with.

As previously stated, Weber's distinction between class and status dimensions is a fruitful one in the analysis of certain systems of inequality, particularly those associated with traditional societies. However, the Weberian perspective cannot be adopted for the analysis of a modern class system without certain qualifications. Many of the alleged inconsistencies between class and status can in fact be seen to rest on a misunderstanding of these concepts, even as defined by Weber. American sociologists in particular have often tended to exaggerate the autonomy of status, usually by failing to distinguish between its various social sources. Enthusiastic acceptance of the multi-dimensional model has blinded many writers to certain serious flaws and ambiguities in Weber's treatment of the problem, and has led to the application of his key concepts to situations to which they are not strictly applicable. None of this is intended to deny that systematic discrepancies between class and status positions are to be found in a modern industrial setting. Indeed, as we shall later see, it is useful to highlight such instances in order to underline our doubts about the more general and rather sweeping claims advanced by the neo-Weberians.

Certain of the difficulties and confusions which abound in discussions of social honour arise from the fact that honour or status has a variety of quite different social sources. The kinds of evaluation which give rise to a prestige hierarchy and a system of deference can be based on very different criteria, not all having the same implications for the stratification order. To give equal weighting to all forms of status evaluation is to give a misleading picture of the distribution of honour and therefore of its significance in the system of rewards. As a way of illustrating this point it will be useful to consider one major source of honour which does have a crucial bearing on the problems under review, namely, the system of status evaluation based upon the occupational order. It has previously been stressed that the occupational order is the primary source not only of material benefits, but also of various social and symbolic benefits. Status can be regarded as one example of an important non-material reward which is unequally distributed; to stand high in the scale of honour is to be awarded certain social advantages and psychic gratification, although this particular kind of inequality has more general significance. Studies of occupational prestige in a variety of Western societies have recorded a high degree of similarity in the rank ordering of positions. Broadly speaking, occupational categories which rank high in the material reward hierarchy also rank high in the status hierarchy; and those which rank low in the former tend to rank low in the latter. In other words, there is a marked congruence in the two dimensions of inequality based on the division of labour. The multi-dimensional view of stratification acknowledges that, empirically, a fairly high degree of congruence between class and status is to be found; what is denied however is that there is any *necessary* consistency between them. Rather, it is suggested that the occupational order generates serious inconsistencies, so that it is possible to point to significant cases of non-alignment in class and status position. Runciman, one of the most persuasive advocates of the multi-dimensional view, offers the following illustration:

Status . . . is concerned with social estimation and prestige, and although it is closely related to class it is not synonymous with it. Whether people recognize each other as social, as opposed to economic, equals is apt to depend on whether they share the same class situation. But this is not necessarily so, as can be easily demonstrated by comparing, for instance, a curate and a bookmaker, or (an example of Orwell's) a naval commander and his grocer.[16]

Here we are invited to understand that each pair of occupations shares the same class position, but not the same status position – the former occupation in each pair enjoying a higher social status. To take an American example, the Gouldners, presenting the same argument, point out that electricians and railroad conductors rank higher economically, but lower in prestige, than schoolteachers and clergymen.[17] Almost any textbook on stratification will yield similar examples of this kind of discrepancy – and in particular, cases of manual occupations which are relatively highly paid, but which rank low in social status.

Now the objection to these alleged examples of rank inconsistency is that they do not reveal discrepancies between *class* and status position at all, but merely between *income* and status position. Income is of course only one of the factors which go to make up overall class position; as we have already seen, no less important are factors like security of employment, promotion opportunities, long-term income prospects, and the general array of social and material advantages which Weber referred to as 'life-chances'. In fact, one of Weber's major contributions to the study of stratification was to broaden Marx's concept of class position by defining it not simply in terms of property ownership but of market advantages in general. When class is defined in this way, it is quite apparent that the usual arguments brought forward in support of the multi-dimensional view are not really tenable. Well-paid manual occupations do *not* in fact typically enjoy a higher class position than modestly paid professions because the latter almost always have certain built-in advantages, often of a long-term kind, over the former. Thus the fact that even the semi-professions or other types of lower white-collar position are accorded higher status than well-paid manual occupations confirms, rather than denies the congruence between class and status. It is thus a little ironic that the neo-Weberian case for the independence of the status dimension should lean so heavily on a narrow usage of the term 'class' (i.e. weekly income) which is almost the antithesis of Weber's own much broader and more useful definition.

There is also an important methodological point at issue here. This concerns the relevance of pointing up exceptional instances to sociological generalizations. Even though it might well be possible to isolate a few examples of occupations which were out of rank alignment, it is by no means clear what contribution this would make to our understanding of the stratification system. Runciman has suggested that 'even a single instance' of class and status inconsistency would be sufficient to clinch the multi-dimensional case and destroy the counter-argument.[18] But if this stringent test were applied to all propositions in the social sciences it is difficult to imagine any one of them surviving. It is of course perfectly reasonable to point up large-scale or systematic exceptions to a general rule, since this can lead to a refinement or modification of the proposition. But there seems to be little theoretical value in claiming minor exceptions to a generalization if these are of a purely random or contingent nature, and so fail to produce further insights or re-formulations. This point will perhaps emerge more clearly when we come to consider genuine cases of systematic discontinuity between class and status dimensions.

For the present we must turn to those approaches to the problem of status which focus upon certain of its *non*-occupational sources. One argument here is that those who rank low in the scale of occupational prestige are often able to improve their overall social standing by taking on certain non-work roles. The most common of the roles referred to are various leadership positions in voluntary associations and the local community. The possibility of building up additional increments of prestige through social interaction in the community thus ensures that social status is not simply a function of the occupational or class structure. Now as a statement about the fact that certain people in low class positions do sometimes enjoy high status in the community this is perfectly acceptable. We have only to think of working-class Lord Mayors. But if we are to understand it as a proposition about the allocation of honour which could be said to be *typical*, then it is a different matter. Numerous studies have demonstrated that leadership positions in voluntary associations and the like are mostly occupied by individuals of high occupational standing. As Bottomore concluded from his inquiry into the membership of such associations in an English town: 'On the evidence available we must acknowledge that the degree of participation in voluntary organizations is correlated with occupational status, and cannot, therefore, be regarded, in general, as contributing independently to the determination of status.'[19] It would seem in fact that high occupational standing is a necessary qualification for election to leadership positions; so that local associations, far from producing an alternative status system to that generated by the occupational order, tend to give rise to miniature reproductions of it. Given this situation, the argument for an independent source of honour based on community interaction is not too convincing. The fact that wholly atypical instances of status acquisition do occur at the local level cannot be said to affect the systematic distribution of honour, any more than the largesse of an eccentric millionaire could be said to affect the systematic distribution of economic rewards.

Most of the shortcomings in the neo-Weberian approach can be traced back to the absence of anything that could be called a theory of the distribution of honour. It is one of the curiosities of Weber's own discussion that despite the importance he assigned to status he offered little account of the factors governing its distribution. Where he does break silence on this vital issue it is in stating that groups or individuals typically acquire honour by 'usurpation' – that is by imitating the life-styles of groups in higher social strata. As he puts it, 'The development of status is essentially a question of stratification resting upon usurpation. Such usurpation is the *normal origin of almost all status honour*.'[20] Clearly this is hardly satisfactory as an explanation of status distribution in a modern social setting. At the very best it is merely a proposition about the manipulation of the status order once it has already become institutionalized. In traditional societies where honour is allocated on the basis of purely ascriptive criteria, usurpation may well often be an important mode of status acquisition. In India, for example, the use of ritual techniques ('sanskritization') as a means of caste mobility appears to be one form of usurpation; another was the social emulation of aristocratic life styles by the mercantile *nouveaux riches* of nineteenth-century Europe. But it is doubtful, to say the very least, whether we could accurately portray the status system of modern Western society in such terms. Certain popular commentators on the human condition would no doubt disagree. Their accounts of affluent consumer behaviour as a manifestation of 'status-seeking' would seem to be a modern dress version of the usurpation thesis. The argument seems to be that the display of expensive consumer goods is an effective technique for laying claim to social honour, particularly on the part of those anxious to preserve or improve their relative status position. Humble men, by acquiring possessions similar to those of men in high positions, can achieve, or attempt to achieve, higher social standing for themselves. This modern usurpation or status-seeking thesis is to be found in its most extravagant guise in the writings of Vance Packard, but it has also received support in the work of academic social theorists, among them Thorstein Veblen and C. Wright Mills.[21]

There is, however, very little evidence that the mere possession or display of valued goods does in fact result in the successful usurpation of honour. Indeed, it is doubtful not only if the display of possessions can effectively bring about changes in relative social standing, but also if this is in fact the primary motive for the accumulation of goods, as is so often suggested by popular commentators. As Lockwood has pointed out, since most of the goods typically acquired by affluent consumers have obvious *practical* utility it makes little sense to see them as purely symbolic objects.[22] If social honour could be acquired in this manner we should expect the status order to be highly fluid and unstable over time as people continually revised one another's social standing in the light of their new possessions or changing consumption patterns. Again, this kind of fluidity may well characterize the status order of certain tribal communities, in which honour is lost and won in the course of competitive exchanges,[23] but it does not realistically portray the situation in our type of society. One of the features of a modern stratification order is that the allocation of honour is governed by certain rules which ensure a high degree of stability in the status system. If honour could be successfully usurped by status-seekers operating outside the framework of these rules, then the very legitimacy of the system would be imperilled.

5

Certain of the difficulties posed by the discussion of social status arise because the term has become overweighted with conceptual cargo. Present usage draws insufficient distinction between, for example, status as a reputational attribute of *persons*, and status as a formal attribute of *positions*. Status as a reputational attribute attaching to particular persons arises on the basis of interaction in face-to-face situations. It is status in this sense which is the main concern of small group analysts, like Blau and Homans.[24]

They represent it as a social increment which individuals build up and sustain through regular encounters with a given set of *alters*; as such it has little or no transferability outside the restricted setting in which it emerges. Reputational status typically arises on the basis of personal evaluations of those who share a similar class position. Sykes's account of social relations among navvies provides us with a colourful illustration of this.

It is noteworthy that individuals could gain a great deal of status among the other navvies by feats of wild behaviour and by building up a reputation as a 'fighting man', a 'drinking man', or a 'gambling man'. As there was a strong oral tradition among the navvies and stories of particular feats were carried from camp to camp and constantly retold to admiring audiences it was possible for a man to acquire a wide reputation throughout the industry. Thus the more famous of the men and the more outstanding foremen and general foremen are known throughout the industry and many stories about them are current . . . Several of the younger men were clearly hoping to 'make a name for themselves' by some feat and thus gain status and recognition in the industry.[25]

Reputational status of this kind would seem to be a common outcome of social interaction among class peers; another well documented example of it would be the distinction often made in working-class communities between 'rough' and 'respectable' families.

This use of the term 'status' and its synonyms to describe the reputational attributes of individuals (which often boil down to personality differences) contrasts with the use of the same term to describe the system of ranked positions which constitutes the national prestige structure. In so far as the study of stratification is primarily concerned with the formal properties of the system of inequalities, then it is status as an attribute of *positions*, not of persons, that must occupy our attention. Status as an attribute of persons is of more relevance to the study of certain other areas of sociology, such as the analysis of small groups or socio-psychological aspects of behaviour. It throws little light on the issues under discussion here. The national prestige structure cannot be understood as an amalgam of the reputational qualities of individuals earned in *gemeinschaftlich* social settings; it is quite independent of small-scale interaction processes and is indeed a phenomenon of an entirely different order. Many writers tend to conflate these quite separate meanings of status, so that evidence relating to the reputational standing of individuals is cited in support of the claim regarding the functional autonomy of the status dimension. Such a failure to distinguish between personal and positional status is perhaps part of the general weakness in the neo-Weberian approach already referred to, namely, the tendency to give all phenomena equal weighting for explanatory purposes. This is a far remove from Weber's own methodology which sought to establish the *patterns* underlying social action and to distinguish these from random and contingent features. It was the concern to illuminate ideal-typical features of inequality which led him to focus on classes and strata, and similar social aggregates, rather than on the attributes of individuals. As we have seen, there is a present tendency to abandon this broad perspective and with it a proper understanding of the system of inequalities. So much is now presented as evidence for the fragmentation of the stratification order, and for class and status inconsistency in particular, that Weber's more rigorous formulations have tended to become somewhat trivialized. This is unfortunate because major cleavages between the dimensions of inequality certainly do exist in modern industrial settings; but they are not singled out as they should be from the more dubious claims we have just examined. To represent the stratification system as a highly fragmented complex of separate and autonomous elements is really to offer few clues as to where the major areas of disjunction are located. Let us now examine briefly some such points of class and status discrepancy and contrast them with the kinds of neo-Weberian claims we have already rejected.

The most obvious and clear-cut example of a major inconsistency between the different dimensions of inequality is that occurring in multi-racial societies. The system of social honour based on ethnic or racial differences is analytically, and often empirically, distinct from that based on the division of labour. Consequently, status positions associated with ethnic ranking are not necessarily in alignment with occupational or class positions. The negative social honour attaching to black minorities in Britain and America, or to the Jews in continental Europe, cannot be explained in class terms. Rather we have to take account of a complex set of cultural and historical factors, such as the institution of slavery, white colonial conquest, the religious persecutions of the Middle Ages, and so on. Powerful historical influences of this kind have by no means been dissolved by the forces of modern industrialism, but have persisted to create a distinct source of status inequality. Status ranking associated with historically rooted ethnic factors is functionally unrelated to the occupational reward system, so that it is not perhaps surprising that we should find serious discrepancies between class and status positions. To cite rather similar examples, certain industrial societies have a system of status ranks based upon the religious cleavage between Catholics and Protestants, as in Ulster, or between different language groups, as in Canada and Belgium. Where such differentiation has also resulted in notions of superiority and inferiority, for whatever historical reasons, then we can expect to find large-scale class and status discrepancies. That is to say, many groups in the society will rank high in social class terms, as measured by their occupational position, but low in social honour as measured by their racial, religious, or language group status. Similarly, or course, the inconsistencies could occur the other way around, as in the case of 'poor whites' in the Deep South, or Protestant labourers in Ulster. Expressed somewhat differently, we could say that members of these 'mixed' societies have two quite different sources of social honour, one deriving from the occupational order and the other from some historically-based system of evaluation. The former rests primarily upon achievement criteria, and the latter upon ascriptive criteria; consequently, they need not necessarily be in close alignment.

Now if the multi-dimensional or neo-Weberian thesis rested squarely upon this type of class and status inconsistency there could be no quarrel with it. But it does not: as we have seen, it embraces a battery of assumptions which are quite separate from those entailed in the present argument. Indeed, the examples of inconsistency just considered give added force to our objections to the indiscriminate use of this notion. For to point up discrepancies in the class and status position of, say, white-collar Jews or Negroes is not to refer to random or exceptional cases, nor to the reputational attributes of individuals. It is, rather, to draw attention to highly structured ambiguities in the life situation of social collectivities, and thus to certain tensions which are felt throughout the stratification order. It is the failure to distinguish this type of situation from other alleged cases of inconsistency which is one of the more disturbing shortcomings of the multi-dimensional approach to the study of stratification.

It has already been suggested that Weber's own views on the relationship between different dimensions of inequality were to some extent coloured by his interest in traditional societies. An important feature of stratification in non-industrial, as against industrial, societies, is that the former tend to show a greater degree of differentiation in the social bases of reward. That is to say, material, social, and symbolic privileges flow from a variety of independent sources. Thus, ownership of land, military prowess and control over arms, the claims to ritual and religious knowledge, the possession of mercantile and commercial skills, or the command of literacy, have often provided quite distinct bases of honour and reward in traditional societies. The institutional separation in feudal society between the powers of the landed nobility, the Church, and the merchant classes is perhaps one of the best documented examples of a diversified or multi-based reward system. In this type of social arrangement, rewards do not flow from a single primary source so that, almost inevitably, discontinuities are to be found between wealth and status positions. The rich but socially despised merchant class of traditional China, or the often impoverished but highly esteemed Brahmins in India, or *Samurai* in Japan, are typical cases in point, and were the kinds of examples Weber drew upon to support his major proposition. Nineteenth-century and early twentieth-century Europe furnished similar instances. Throughout Europe at this time families of noble lineage enjoyed considerable social and economic influence, despite their gradual loss of formal political authority. The possession of great landed wealth rendered them relatively immune from the pressures of industrialism, and enabled them to maintain a style of life revolving around the pursuit of leisure and courtly entertainment. The aristocracy stood at the apex of the status order and succeeding in upholding a system of honour based on the purely ascriptive principles of descent. Below the ranks of the aristocracy the status order was geared more closely to the industrial and occupational order. A major point of tensions in this dual system, well illustrated by Weber's formulation, occurred in the attempt by groups which had become materially successful in the world of industry or commerce to enter the aristocratic status order. The tendency for aspiring *nouveau riche* families to attempt to cleanse their wealth by courting the acceptance of, and marriage into, families of noble pedigree was a characteristic feature of the European class system at this time. These attempts were not always successful, so producing similar kinds of discrepancies between wealth and status to those found in non-industrial societies.

However, a marked development in European social structure since Weber's time has been the rapid decline in the fortunes and social influence of the landed nobility. The loss of estates in the period between the two world wars finally removed the material base which had supported a distinct and identifiable leisure class at the apex of industrial society.[26] By mid-century at latest it would no longer have been accurate to portray the status order as a dual system with two distinct sets of criteria for allocating honour. Even in those European countries where the Monarchy survived war and revolution, Royalty no longer served as a point of anchorage for aristocratic life styles, but tended instead to celebrate solid *bourgeois* virtues and the splendours of family life. Where in modern Europe the aristocracy has survived it has tended to adapt itself to the new industrial order, either by entering the formerly despised worlds of trade, commerce, and banking, or by becoming professionally qualified, or, in England, by becoming public showmen. This decline in the fortunes of the aristocracy in the twentieth century has accelerated the tendency for the reward structure to become less diversified, and for the occupational order to impose a much more unitary stamp upon it. And as the occupational order comes increasingly to be the primary source of symbolic as well as material advantages, so the areas for potential discrepancy between the different dimensions of inequality tend to diminish. Serious discrepancies can, as we have seen, still be expected to occur in societies where historically based racial or religious

39

cleavages promote an autonomous system of moral evaluation; it certainly cannot be argued that the forces of industrial change will necessarily bring about any uniformity of rewards in this respect. However, the fact that these trends are likely to persist in 'mixed' societies should not obscure the equally important fact that industrial societies do have a more unitary reward system than do non-industrial societies. And it is for this, if for no other, reason that a multi-dimensional model of stratification has to be handled with particular caution.

6

The appeal of Weber's work on stratification has rested to a large extent on the importance he accorded to subjective factors. The role assigned to evaluative processes has been central to the critique of Marx's view of the class structure; and the widespread attraction of subjectivist notions among latter-day sociologists is not unrelated to scholarly attempts to refute the 'materialist' argument. However it must be said that the subjectivist case is open to serious doubt at many points, and has in fact done much to encourage a quite misleading view of the relationship between material inequality and the status order.

Most of the key assumptions underlying the subjectivist position are brought out in studies of occupational prestige. Occupational prestige scales are constructed by aggregating the status evaluations of a representative sample of the population. The ranking of positions which results from this exercise is then held to indicate the common view on matters of prestige. This is what might be called the 'moral referendum' view of social honour; the assumption is that the prestige accorded to different positions derives from the sum total of individual assessments, rather in the way that the Top Ten music chart is constructed from the total selections of individual record buyers. Such a procedure thus leads to the view that the distribution of social honour is regarded as legitimate (whatever may be felt about the distribution of material reward) because it rests upon popular evaluations of common worth. 'Status evaluations require community consensus as to the standards that are to be used. Most important, status . . . can derive only from the respect and honour that others are willing to give. Therefore status has a highly personal quality, quite unlike the impersonal and rational quality that determines classes.'[27] In similar vein, the major British study of occupational ranking concluded that there was 'a substantial measure of public agreement as to the prestige of various occupations'.[28] One of the best-known American inquiries into prestige ranking, *Jobs and Occupations*, conducted by the National Opinion Research Center, is subtitled, 'A Popular Evaluation', which again indicates its general line of approach to the problem.[29]

However, it is by no means always clear from these empirical studies whether what is being measured is the individual's own personal evaluation of the social worth of various positions, or simply his assessment of what he takes to be the *factual* social standing of these positions. Because we are well aware of an existent status hierarchy, any judgements we are required to make are bound to be affected by our knowledge of how the actual rank order works in everyday life. Thus, the fact that so many ranking studies report a high level of 'general agreement' should not necessarily be taken as an index of popular feeling regarding matters of status; what is often being measured is the perception of the existent status hierarchy, and not our own private evaluations of the way positions *ought* to be socially ranked, if indeed they ought to be ranked at all. The point is, that if studies of occupational prestige are mainly tapping the general awareness of an existing state of affairs, then such findings clearly cannot be used to support the 'moral referendum' view of status distribution. That is, we cannot say, on the basis of such evidence, that status *derives* from popular evaluations of the moral worth of different positions. Such findings tell us not about the sources of social honour but about the popular perception of its factual distribution. To explain the distribution itself we need a rather different approach.

It is here that Marx, although he was little concerned with matters of status as such, would appear to be a more useful guide than Weber. Expressing one of Marx's major propositions in somewhat un-Marxist terms, it is plausible to regard social honour as an emergent property generated by the class system. More concisely, we can consider it as a system of social evaluation arising from the moral judgements of those who occupy dominant positions in the class structure. In this sense there is an obvious subjective aspect to it. But the important point is that it is not the moral evaluations of the population at large which give rise to the status system, but mainly the evaluations of dominant class members. It is the latter's definitions of social and moral worth which take on factual embodiment, thereby establishing the main framework of the status order. Marx's claim that 'the ideas of the ruling class are, in every age, the ruling ideas', rests upon the fact that those who control the major agencies of socialization typically occupy privileged class positions. As a consequence, their definitions of social reality, and their moral judgements, are far more likely to be blessed with the stamp of public legitimacy than are the social and moral constructs of those in subordinate class positions.

To suggest that the system of status is dependent upon the normative socialization of one class by another is not to claim that the formal ranking of occupations is ever itself the subject of social indoctrination. There is little that we could call explicit socialization regarding the placement of various positions in the status hierarchy. Clearly, this could not be so, given the many thousands of occupations involved. Thus it is not the ranking of occupations as such which is formally upheld by the socialization process; rather it is the *criteria* by which positions are to be ranked. That is to say, certain criteria become institutionalized as 'relevant' for ranking purposes, while other criteria are excluded or defined as 'irrelevant'. Once a given set of rank criteria has been successfully legitimized throughout society, then the main lines of the status order will have been laid down. Obviously, the number of logically possible rank criteria is quite large, so that many different ways of socially grading the same positions are feasible. If, for example, occupational prestige were allocated on the basis of the physical effort, or danger or dirtiness of the tasks performed, it would result in a quite different status order from that in which technical expertise, skill, or responsibility were held to be the relevant rank criteria. In our type of society, rank criteria of the latter kind are accorded much greater legitimacy and institutional backing than are criteria of the former kind; hence professional occupations are assigned a high position in the prestige order while labouring occupations are assigned a low place. This means that it is not necessary for members of society to have a detailed knowledge of different occupations in order to be able to place them mentally in the prestige hierarchy. All that is necessary is that they should have some rough idea of whether or not any given occupation is endowed with the 'relevant' rank attributes. For example, as Kriesberg's study has suggested, there is a tendency for people to accord high rank to any occupation they take to be a professional one; this is because even though they may know little or nothing about the occupation in question, they know that professions *in general* enjoy high status.[30] In other words we could say that institutionalized rank criteria provide a framework of occupational stereotypes or categories into which any occupation can be incorporated.

Although the factual status system can be said to be part of the package deal of normative socialization, it need not be argued that the rank criteria upheld by the dominant class are fully accepted as legitimate by all sectors of the subordinate class. There is in fact evidence that many members of the latter class employ different criteria when asked to rank positions according to their own personal standards of worth. Young and Willmott's study of social grading by manual workers in London reported that many respondents reversed the factual rank order by assigning high status to manual occupations and low status to non-manual ones.[31] They did this by emphasizing social usefulness as one of their main criteria of moral worth, and by devaluing the dominant criteria of education, skill, and authority position. It was made clear by the authors of the study, however, that only a minority of workers adopted 'deviant' criteria in their assessments; the majority tended to employ the rank criteria upheld by the dominant class, and so reproduced the orthodox status hierarchy. This finding suggests that major segments of the subordinate class endorse a system of honour which puts a negative evaluation on their own class. And although a minority may reject this state of affairs when asked to express a personal view, it seems likely that they too would be constrained to *act* according to the norms of the factual status order, particularly in their social encounters with members of the dominant class. To do otherwise, especially of course in the work situation, could produce sharp negative reactions.

In so far, then, as there seems to be a general agreement about the factual status order and its day-to-day operation, it would be more realistic to see it as a tribute to the effectiveness of the socialization process than as evidence for some sort of moral consensus independently arrived at by different class members. The latter view could not explain why the distribution of honour was governed by one set of rank criteria rather than another. It thus fails to make explicit the full significance of the relationship between social status and the class structure. It is a feature of every stratification system that those who occupy the dominant positions seek to ensure that the main attibutes of their own positions become widely accepted as the appropriate criteria for allocating honour, and that attributes they do not possess become defined as irrelevant for ranking purposes. If the distribution of honour failed to match the distribution of material advantages, the system of inequalities would be stripped of its normative support. How could sharp differences in material reward be formally justified if it was widely held that all occupations were of equal social value? A major function of the prestige order is to deny this latter premise. It thereby serves to stabilize and legitimize inequalities by harnessing notions of social justice in defence of existing class privileges. Clearly, such an interpretation of the meaning of social status is fundamentally opposed to that which treats it as an independent dimension of inequality arising from subjective assessments of social worth.

7

Finally, to suggest as we have that the system of honour is imposed on society by a dominant class is to come face-to-face with the thorny problem of power. We are confronted in particular with the task of considering whether or to what extent power itself is to be thought of as a separate dimension of stratification. As in the case of status, discussions of power tend to be bedevilled by the rich variety of meanings with which the term is endowed, both in everyday and in sociological discourse. Thus, for many writers power is simply the ability of X to achieve desired ends, notwithstanding opposition from Y, whether X and Y refer to groups or to individuals. In small group studies, for example, *ego* is said to have power over *alter* to the extent that he can successfully manipulate encounters between them to his own net advantage. In this sense we could speak of the power of a mistress over her infatuated lover, or of the power of a stronger personality over a weaker one, and so on. Power here could be regarded as an element which enters to some degree in almost any kind of interpersonal transaction, and as such it is virtually impossible to generalize about its social distribution. This usage of the term is a quite common and acceptable one, and the kinds of issue it seeks to illuminate are of genuine sociological interest. But it should at once be apparent that it is a usage which has little relevance to the problems here being considered.

A second usage of the term is that which treats it as an attribute of office. Here power, or authority, derives from the incumbency of positions in hierarchical organizations. We can plot its distribution quite readily because it flows in accordance with the pyramidal arrangement of positions in formal institutional settings. Thus X has power over Y not on the basis of personality differences, nor because of situational contingencies, but because X enjoys higher office than Y. With this usage we move nearer to the subject matter of stratification in so far as attention is directed to the structure of positions. For some writers, most notably Dahrendorf and Burnham, office power is the key variable in determining class structure in modern industrial society.[32] Those who occupy command positions are, by virtue of this fact, held to be in a different and usually antagonistic class position from those who occupy positions lacking authority. Seen from this angle, class inequality and class conflict emerge from the unequal distribution not of material resources but of authority roles. The central objection to this view is that it describes the cleavages within formal or bureaucratic organizations, but not cleavages which occur at the *societal* level. By Dahrendorf's reckoning, every single large-scale organization has a dominant and subordinate 'class'; administration and students in university, clergy and laity in the Church, warders and inmates in prisons, managers and workers in factories, and so forth. But obviously the lines of authority which cut across each formal organization do not interlock, as it were, to form a major cleavage cutting across society. We could not regard university administrators, prison warders, Church officials, factory managers, and the like, as comprising a single dominant class in opposition to a single subordinate class composed of those lacking any form of office power. Again, then, although this usage of the term is quite fruitful for the analysis of organizations, and of conflicts within organizations, it is not especially helpful in the study of stratification at the societal level.

Once we come to consider power as an aspect of stratification, and not simply of role differentiation, we cannot easily separate it from the material and symbolic elements of inequality already examined. To some extent, in fact, to conceive of stratification in terms of power may simply be another way of conceptualizing the distribution of class and status advantages. That is, to speak of the distribution of power could be understood as another way of describing the flow of rewards; the very fact that the dominant class can successfully claim a disproportionate share of rewards *vis-à-vis* the subordinate class, is in a sense a *measure* of the former's power over the latter. In other words, power need not be thought of as something which exists over and above the system of material and social rewards; rather, it can be thought of as a concept or metaphor which is used to depict the flow of resources which constitutes this system. And as such it is not a separate dimension of stratification at all. Weber himself advocated this way of looking at the matter by claiming that '"classes", "status groups" and "parties" are *phenomena of the distribution of power* within a community'.[33]

It would seem in fact to be the neo-Weberians, rather than Weber himself, who single out power as a distinct element of stratification. As the above quotation shows, Weber's emphasis was on the role of the political *party* as a separate dimension of the reward structure. This is an altogether different point, and one which draws attention to an important issue; namely, the relationship between class inequality and mass political parties designed to redress the balance of advantages in favour of the subordinate class. In the following chapters we shall have cause to take up this issue from a number of angles. In Chapter 4 we examine the impact made upon the stratification system by governments based on Social Democratic parties in capitalist societies. In Chapter 5 we ask similar questions of societies in which the Communist Party occupies the seat of power. Before this, however, we must turn our attention to a somewhat different set of issues. In the next chapter we consider some of the more important social factors which serve to stabilize the existing structure of inequality, and in Chapter 3 we examine certain of the normative systems which provide competing definitions of the meaning of inequality.

2   Social Sources of Stability

Inequality in the distribution of rewards is always a potential source of political and social instability. Because upper, relatively advantaged strata are generally fewer in number than disadvantaged lower strata, the former are faced with crucial problems of social control over the latter. One way of approaching this issue is to ask not why the disprivileged often rebel against the privileged but why they do not rebel more often than they do. In this way we can examine some of the social mechanisms which stabilize the stratification order and help to maintain the system of inequalities intact. A few industrial societies have solved this problem in a fairly crude and straightforward way; by the use or threat of physical coercion. The Soviet Union under Stalin, or South Africa at the present time, are examples of societies which have relied heavily on repressive means to maintain the distribution of privileges. This situation, though, is fairly uncommon among modern industrial societies. Even in social systems founded on the use of force, attempts are always made to win the hearts and minds of the populace. Thus, one of the central aims of any dominant class is to make the rules governing the distribution of rewards seem legitimate in the eyes of all, including those who stand to gain least from such rules. The greater the extent to which this is achieved, the more stable the political order is likely to be, and the less need for recourse to coercive means.

Elements of consensus and coercion are, of course, present in the control system of every society, although the actual balance between the two elements varies from one society to another. It is useful to bear in mind that even in the most apparently benevolent societies the state has important functions of coercion and control, as well as of welfare. Direct internal threats to the institutions supporting inequality often bring into play the physical forces which, ultimately, are designed to protect these institutions. Inside the velvet glove of any state is always an iron fist. The complexities of modern class-stratified societies cannot properly be understood unless the existence of both glove and fist are acknowledged.

For the most part, as we have said, the use of physical coercion is not commonly necessary to control members of the underclass. There are a variety of less drastic social mechanisms, mostly not deliberately created by the dominant class, which have a safety-valve effect on the stratification order. One of the more important of these safety-valves, and one having a number of political implications, is the process of social mobility.

2

All industrial societies exhibit a certain amount of social exchange between classes from one generation to the next. The degree of openness or fluidity in the class system naturally varies between societies or in any one society over time. But as a rough general estimate, between about a quarter and a third of those born into the manual working class in modern Western countries will move into the ranks of the middle class. In the socialist societies of Eastern Europe the chances for social promotion have generally been somewhat greater than this, due mainly to a series of far-reaching educational reforms. But whatever political complexion the society has, opportunities for a considerable minority of the least privileged class to achieve more favourable positions appear to be built into it. This is partly to do with the expansion of white-collar occupations in the tertiary sector of the economy, and continuous technological innovation. But also of importance is the fact that the middle class does not usually reproduce itself sufficiently – in the sense of providing enough offspring – to staff all the new positions. Where white-collar positions are in excess of the number of able middle-class personnel, there is bound to be some attempt to recruit the most talented members of the underclass. This creaming-off process is especially necessary when new positions are thought to demand measurable talents and abilities. Those born into the dominant class cannot then assume privileged positions as of right in the way that they can in systems where proof of talent or ability is not required. Once the criteria for assessing ability have become institutionalized the well born often find themselves in competition with gifted or ambitious members from lower social strata. Thus, even if the expansion of white-collar positions should tail off, and the middle class *could* replenish itself from its own offspring, upward recruitment and competition from below could still be expected to occur. But whether, in such a situation, we should get the wholesale displacement of those born to privilege, to make room for the more talented, is a matter of some doubt. This is a point we shall return to later in this chapter.

The political implications of upward social mobility seem apparent enough. Mobility provides an escape route for large numbers of the most able and ambitious members of the underclass, thereby easing some of the tensions generated by inequality. Elevation into the middle class represents a *personal* solution to the problems of low status, and as such tends to weaken collectivist efforts to improve the lot of the underclass as a whole. It has often been suggested that upward mobility undermines the political base of the underclass most seriously by siphoning off the men best fitted for leadership. The continuous drain of talent may well be a source of political weakness, but we should not exaggerate its effects upon working-class movements and institutions. The process of educational and occupational selection is by no means efficient enough to skim off all available talent. In the absence of a pure meritocracy great numbers of gifted men do not move into middle-class positions and there appears to be no obvious shortage of potential leaders. Furthermore, the kinds of abilities measured by intelligence and aptitude tests, and which make for occupational advancement, may well differ from the kinds of abilities required of political leaders. Only if the necessary qualities were the same in both cases would the drain of talent be serious.

Again, a certain amount of caution is called for in considering the political effects of upward mobility brought about by the changing outlook of those who cross the class line. There is little doubt that the overall tendency is for the upwardly mobile to shift their political allegiances from parties of the Left to parties of the Right. Not very much is yet known about this process from a personal angle, but we can plausibly assume it to be part of the individual's general readjustment to the values of his class of destination. A switch in political outlook from, say, Labour to Conservative may be understood as one stage in the re-definition of the self which tends to follow social promotion, and which may indeed be a necessary condition for the successful maintenance of, and adjustment to, a new class position. We could of course expect that the degree of personal adjustment would be related to the amount of social distance travelled. It is likely that social promotion into the ranks of the professional and managerial middle class would call for a more thorough-going overhaul of political and social identity than would recruitment to humbler, routine white-collar positions. Support for parties of the Right becomes more pronounced the higher we ascend in the non-manual hierarchy, and it is likely that adherence to typically working-class political loyalties would be more difficult with every upward step.[1] This would be especially true of middle-class occupations centred in the world of business and commerce and finance, where loyalty to the political values of the Right is particularly fierce. In Western societies with high rates of '*élite*' or long-range upward mobility, then, we should expect a considerable attrition of political radicalism.

Most social mobility, however, is of a relatively short-range kind and so does not necessarily involve sharp changes in political identity. The children of manual workers who cross the class line tend to assume fairly modest white-collar positions – as clerks, salesmen, shop assistants, schoolteachers, and the like. Recruitment to established middle-class professions requiring long periods of training and education is far less common. The usual pattern of short-range mobility would not be expected to lead to the serious erosion of working-class values and political loyalties. In most Western European countries support for Social Democratic parties is quite common among members of lower white-collar occupations, especially salaried employees on state and local government payrolls – a sector of the middle class which is also notably susceptible to the appeals of unionization. Many lower white-collar employees are of working-class origin and it is reasonable to assume that a good number have imported into the middle class certain of the political values commonly held in their former class.

There is some evidence to suggest that even among the upwardly mobile who transfer their *party* allegiance from Left to Right, adherence to certain collectivist and egalitarian values is quite common.[2] This suggests that party identifications are more easily shed by the mobile than are attitudes to inequality. A change in voting behaviour and party support may be an acceptable token of adjustment to a new station in life; but it appears to be one which is not necessarily accompanied by the wholesale abandonment of political beliefs formed during the period of early socialization in the underclass. If the upwardly mobile supporters of the Right differ in political outlook from supporters of the Right born into the middle class – and the evidence suggests they do – then we must treat the 'de-radicalization' thesis with some caution. Because although upward mobility may cause a certain Rightward shift in party identification, one effect of this is likely to be a change in the normative basis of support for the Right. This process could be one of the many factors associated with the acceptance by Conservative parties of various welfare and collectivist policies. Although these policies are usually championed by working-class parties they also appear to have a certain amount of appeal to lower white-collar groups. We could reasonably speculate that the upwardly mobile would be well represented among the latter, whatever their formal political party attachments. Thus, against the process of political '*embourgeoisement*', so frequently stressed, we must set the equally marked tendency in the opposite direction, namely, what we might call the 'proletarianization' of certain sectors of the middle class. We should guard against the view that the upwardly mobile are simply moulded into political shape by the pressures of the stratification system. This system itself, and its political character, can in turn be modified by those who cross from one class to the next. At the same time, this is not to deny the validity of the broad view that opportunities for social promotion do release some of the tensions inherent in a stratified system, and so serve as a mechanism for stabilizing the political order.

If upward mobility is a political safety-valve, what of downward mobility? Many industrial societies are shown to have higher rates of downward than upward mobility.[3] In Britain, for example, over 40 per cent of those born in the non-manual class can expect to drop into the manual working class. Many other Western societies show comparable rates of downward movement. Potentially, wholesale social demotion could be regarded as a likely source of political unrest. Those born into the middle class and accustomed to its security and privileges might be expected to feel little love for a social order which dropped them into the rather more severe environment of the manual working class. There are certainly some indications that those who have slipped in the social scale are somewhat more disenchanted with their lot than those whose position has not deteriorated. But on the whole, the expression of discontent does not take an overtly political form, at least in the sense of hostility to, or rejection of, the social order. The evidence from most countries is that the downwardly mobile do not change their political allegiances to correspond to those typical of their class of destination. Wilensky found that downwardly mobile men in the United States were also far more likely to think of themselves as 'middle class' or even 'upper class' than were manual workers born in the working class.[4] 81 per cent of the latter thought of themselves as lower or working class, as against only 46 per cent of the former. Furthermore, the 'skidders', as Wilensky calls the downwardly mobile, were more likely to subscribe to the belief in an open class system, and that plentiful opportunities for advancement were available to men of ability. Unlike most men born of working-class families they anticipated leaving factory employment in the near future in favour of some form of white-collar employment. Lipset and Gordon, in their study of workers in San Francisco, found similar variations in the attitudes of skidders and the rest. Skidders were more resistant to the appeals of trade unionism than were other workers, as well as more optimistic about the chances for social promotion.[5] British workers, too, are more likely to consider themselves middle class if their fathers were in white-collar rather than manual positions – a factor associated with support for the Conservative Party.[6]

Thus, if upward mobility is frequently accompanied by a political shift from Left to Right, there is little in the way of a compensating shift in the opposite direction among the downwardly mobile. It is not, of course, too surprising that the socially demoted should be somewhat more reluctant to jettison their former political identity than are the socially ascendant. Recruitment into the middle class entails a re-defining of the self in a more favourable light – as judged by prevailing standards of moral worth. Social descent, on the other hand, results in a potentially more damaging confrontation between self and social reality, a confrontation which people are likely to avoid, or at least to ease, whenever they can. One way of doing this is through the belief that the fall from grace is a temporary affair, and that one's former status will eventually be recaptured – if only through the success of one's children. To sever symbolic ties with the political representatives of the middle class would in a sense be a sign of having accepted lower social status as a permanent fate, instead of a short-lived interlude. Again, to reject the middle-class vision of society as an open opportunity structure, in which effort and ability are duly rewarded, would be equally damaging, since belief in such a system fertilizes the hope of eventual social redemption. It is among the socially demoted that status anxieties could be expected to be especially acute, and immersion into working-class life and institutions strongly resisted. Far from embracing the political values and social outlook of their class of destination, there is some evidence that the downwardly mobile tend often to become somewhat more Right-wing than the middle class as a whole. High rates of downward mobility are thus not as threatening to the stratification order as might have been predicted. Part of the reason for this is that those who have been socialized into middle-class values have individualistic rather than collectivist leanings. Their responses to downward mobility tend, therefore, to involve some form of personal adjustment or recovery, and not a demand to change the system of rewards through communal action. If massive downward mobility were allied with strong collectivist views a potentially

more explosive situation would be liable to result. As Wilensky
has put it:

Skidders, along with other workers who escape from working class
culture psychologically or actually, function to reduce working class
solidarity and social criticism from below – and thereby slow down
the push toward equality. But if the déclassé were not optimistic-
grateful, they might combine with normally apathetic workers to
form the vanguard of extremist political movements.[7]

An equally important reason why large-scale downward
movement is fairly easily 'contained' by the political order is
that, as in the case of upward movement, most of it takes place
over a relatively narrow social distance. Although the skidders
are likely to experience some social discomfort from their experience, for most of them the actual drop in material and social
standing would not be catastrophic. The step from lower middle
class to skilled or 'respectable' working class (where most of them
arrive) is not a very big one, at least as measured by the usual
economic and social criteria. Nor again could there be said to be
a sharp cultural hiatus between the lower ranks of the middle
class and the upper ranks of the working class. Patterns of
family life, entertainment and leisure activities, consumer-goods
expenditure, level of education, patterns of speech, and the like,
are not markedly different for the two groups. No doubt this is
partly to do with the process of upward mobility already referred
to, which results in the incorporation of certain elements of
working-class culture into the non-manual stratum. In fact, in
societies with relatively high rates of both upward and downward mobility at the margins of the class divide, it is probable
that a large proportion of families will have members in both
blue-collar and white-collar occupations. In Britain, for example,
it certainly is not unusual to have some kin members – siblings,
close cousins, or affines – in a different social class from oneself.
This is brought about, partly, by a social practice whose relative
frequency is in itself a useful index of cultural similarity; namely,
intermarriage across class lines. There is a good deal of social
exchange between the classes through marriage, the slight
tendency being for women to marry 'up' and men to marry
'down'. It should again be emphasized, however, that most of

this interchange takes place on the margins of the class frontier, and does not commonly involve the union of families separated by broad stretches of social space.

We could sum up these remarks by suggesting that there is what might be called a social and cultural 'buffer zone' between the middle class and working class proper. Most mobility, being of a fairly narrow social span, involves the movement into and out of this zone rather than movement between the class extremes. This is one important reason why mobility would not generally give rise to adjustment problems of a very acute nature. The patterns of behaviour and social symbolism of the 'respectable' working class would not be especially disturbing or foreign to a typical member of the lower middle class, especially if he had kinsmen or his own family roots in the working class. It seems probable that a great deal of what counts as social mobility is simply the marginal class fluctuations of members of the same families from one generation to the next. And if the downwardly mobile can recover lost ground in the next generation by ensuring their children's success, then their own social demotion may be less keenly felt. Evidence that they are quite adept at recovering former status on behalf of their children is certainly not lacking. A variety of studies has shown that working-class children who have at least one parent of middle-class origin tend to do noticeably better at school than working-class children whose parents have had no middle-class family experience. Women who have been downwardly mobile through marriage to working-class men appear to play an especially important role in the advancement of their own children. Elizabeth Cohen's study of American working-class high-school boys showed that, among her sample, 80 per cent of those whose mothers were of white-collar family background were going to college, compared with only 42 per cent of those whose mothers were of working-class origin.[8] Given the crucial link between level of educational success and occupational achievement, we can take this as evidence of higher potential for upward mobility on the part of working-class children whose mothers have been downwardly mobile. More direct evidence for this has been offered by studies which show that working-class children who are propelled upwards into non-manual occupations, through educational achievement, tend to have parents either of middle-class origin, or who are in various ways marginal to the working class. They are families typical of what Jackson and Marsden have called the 'sunken middle class', rather than of the traditional working class of many generations' standing.[9]

As we have said, it is this ability of downwardly mobile families to move up again in the next generation which not only accounts for much of the interchange between classes, but also eases some of the tensions of social demotion. If massive downward mobility were not largely confined to movement of this kind it would be likely to have more serious political repercussions. Members of the professional and managerial middle class, and their offspring, who descended into the manual working class would suffer more of a social shock than would members of lower white-collar occupations. The style of life, work experience, and level of reward of manual workers would entail a quite fundamental readjustment for most of those accustomed to the status and privileges of the established middle class. Long-distance social descent of this kind does, of course, occur in industrial societies, but usually on a fairly modest scale. For the most part, professional middle-class families are able to ensure that their offspring inherit some kind of white-collar status. This they do by providing them with a good education and a home environment conducive to achievement, or, rather less commonly, by the transference of private property. Comparatively little is known about the small number who fall from the upper reaches of the middle class into the manual working class. Some who make the long downward journey appear to be social casualties of one kind or another: for example, the mentally ill or defective, or alcoholics, or those who have various kinds of personal disability which prevent them from holding down a middle-class occupation. In more recent times the *voluntary* relinquishment of middle-class status and style of life has occurred among some of the well-born young in affluent Western societies. But although 'drop-outs' could reasonably be regarded as examples of long-range downward mobility, not sufficient is yet known about their moral careers over a long time-span for us to count them as irretrievably lost to their class of origin. There are some sketchy indications that for many the attractions of Bohemia are fairly short-lived, and that as youth wears off the rewards and comforts of the *bourgeois* world begin to exert an irresistible pull. But at what point drop-outs enter or re-enter the occupational hierarchy, and whether their temporary absence tells against them in the long run, are questions which cannot yet be answered.

Not all long-range downward mobility is to be accounted for by social pathology and the voluntary withdrawal from society. Meritocratic principles doubtless have a sufficient toe-hold to ensure that some at least of the untalented offspring of well-placed parents find themselves in poorly rewarded manual occupations. But it is not altogether surprising that the proportion who make this kind of social descent is fairly small. Given the cultural, educational, and environmental cosseting which children of the upper or professional middle class generally receive, we should expect even the dullest of them to acquire a sufficient gloss of learning, as well as all-important social skills, to fit them for some kind of respectable white-collar job, however routine and humble. At any rate there would appear to be certain difficulties in institutionalizing merit or ability as the sole criteria for allocating men to different positions in the rewards structure. As we mentioned at the beginning of this chapter, tensions over recruitment to favourable positions are not likely to be very acute where such positions are numerous enough to accommodate gifted members of the underclass without seriously jeopardizing the chances of the native-born middle class. But we could hypothesize that tensions would increase if and when the number of advantaged positions fell greatly below the number of middle-class youths entering the labour market. If measured ability were the sole criterion for educational and occupational selection this would make the position of the dominant class more precarious, since their own children would be faced with stiff competition from the most gifted children in the underclass. Thus, in a pure meritocracy the ability of the dominant class to replenish itself from its own kind would be considerably reduced. As industrial societies attempt to improve efficiency by the most rational deployment of talent, certain strains appear to be set up in the stratification order. These occur because the pressures to use human talent efficiently, by rewarding merit, are countered by pressures making for social continuity in the class position of fathers and sons. It would probably be a mistake to assume that the drive towards industrial efficiency will see the complete victory of meritocratic principles. This would assume that members of the dominant class have little control over events, that they are simply swept along by inexorable forces of economic progress. But where privilege goes hand-in-hand with power it may be possible for the most advantaged members of the dominant class to defend their position – for example, by changing the criteria of recruitment in a way beneficial to themselves and their offspring. One way of doing this is, for example, by making the assessment of 'character' an important part of the selection process. Because the kinds of personal attributes that go to make up character are not generally open to objective measurement, the assessment of such attributes can be made by the occupants of privileged positions. To insist on character qualifications, and not simply evidence of 'mere' ability, is a method of controlling access to positions. This is because the kinds of qualities defined as 'good' are more likely than not to be those possessed by members of the dominant class, and the product of a certain kind of social training. In socialist societies, a comparable means of offsetting the claims of ability is to insist upon the equal importance of 'political reliability'. Obviously, the ability to control entry to the best positions is much weakened when merit alone is the deciding factor.

The conflict between demands for the most rational use of talent and the pressures making for class inheritance are present in all modern industrial societies; but this conflict has not so far reached a critical point because there is no shortage of desirable white-collar positions. In fact in most Western societies the demand for essentially middle-class skills appears to be increasing. It has been among some of the under-developed countries, paradoxically enough, that the supply of white-collar personnel has often outstripped demand. Large-scale graduate unemployment, and the political repercussions that tend to follow in its wake, is comparatively rare in the highly industrialized nations. It may, though, be pertinent to wonder at what point in the growth of advanced societies the middle class will cease to expand at the expense of the industrial workforce. Presumably there is some point below which the productive base must cease to shrink if it is to continue to support a burgeoning non-manual sector. It could of course turn out to be the case that a highly automated technology employing a very small labour force would be able to meet all the productive needs of society. But if or when this stage is reached the conventional blue-collar/white-collar dichotomy will probably be of fading significance, since automated production generally demands the type of supervisory skills associated with non-manual rather than manual positions. We should then perhaps have to revise our measures of social mobility and the political generalizations based upon the conventional class divisions.

Social mobility of course affects the fortunes of only a minority of the underclass. The majority of those born into this class will remain in it, and their children will follow in their footsteps. It is among this numerically large sector of the population that we might reasonably expect moral commitment to the political and social order to be at its weakest. Where the burdens of low status are not palliated by prospects of individual improvement, the turn towards collective solutions may become an attractive alternative. Radical political movements aimed at dissolving or reversing the system of inequalities have emerged among the disprivileged in almost all capitalist societies. But although socialist and Marxist movements have drawn most of their strength from lower social strata, particularly the industrial workforce, the turn to radicalism is by no means a necessary, or even typical, response to deprivation. Various other alternatives are also open, most of which constitute no challenge to the political system. It is to a brief examination of some of these that we now turn.

One of the commonest responses to deprivation is that of resignation and acceptance. In traditional societies, especially, those lowest in the social order have more often expressed their feelings by a sense of fatalism than by active resentment. In industrial societies, lower strata have been rather less willing to accept the inevitability of their situation, and are certainly much less prone to regard it as just and legitimate. Nevertheless, despite the emergence of political values and movements which have challenged the basis of inequality, strategies of accommodation and acceptance of low social position are still a marked feature of underclass life. Those who are aware that they occupy a humble place in the hierarchy of rewards are often inclined to tailor their expectations of life to a correspondingly modest level. When expectations are low, the frustration caused by unsatisfied wants is more easily avoided. Dissatisfaction is kept lower than it might be because people tend not to compare their lot with others who are far more highly rewarded than themselves, but rather with those in similar circumstances. Often it seems there is a marked lack of awareness of the extent of inequality on the part of lower status groups. Runciman's study of attitudes to inequality in England showed that a great many people in the low income bracket (those earning less than £15 a week in 1962) thought there were no others better off than themselves.[10] This was not necessarily because they were ignorant of the fact that middle-class professional people like doctors, lawyers, professors, company directors and the like, earned considerably more than they did. Rather, as Runciman suggests, it is because professional white-collar groups are too far removed socially to provide a relevant point of comparison for manual workers. The fact that well rewarded white-collar groups are outside the social vision, as it were, of most manual workers means that the latter do not necessarily feel deprived relative to the former, despite the obvious disparity in their material standing. It is significant, too, that workers who *were* conscious of others being better off than themselves tended on the whole not to perceive the discrepancies in class terms. They were instead likely to single out instances unrelated to class characteristics, such as, 'people on night work', 'people without children', and so on.[11] There appeared to be little recognition of the wide and systematic material disparities generated by a class-stratified society. The objective conditions of inequality are in fact much greater than might be predicted from subjective assessments of the situation. If there were a more realistic appraisal and understanding of the class distribution of rewards the level of discontent among lower strata might well increase. Political radicals attempt to bring this about by demonstrating the extent of material inequality and relating it to the class system. They attempt, in Runciman's terms, to extend the manual workers' reference group to include the highly privileged, thereby heightening the former's sense of relative deprivation.

It should at this point be said that the notion of reference group is quite useful for conceptualizing the problem of lower status responses to the facts of inequality; but it does nevertheless present us with a problem. The problem is to decide whether the selection of narrow-range reference groups on the part of the disprivileged is a cause of their modest expectations, or simply a consequence of these expectations. We could just as easily say that the choice of reference group is largely influenced by the individual's *prior* level of expectations. Those whose expectations and likely achievements are of a modest order might well choose not to compare their lot with the more advantaged, since such comparisons would be upsetting. In other words it could be suggested that the inability of the less privileged to 'see' the more privileged is a protective strategy developed by those *already* resigned to a life of small rewards. This seems to be a more plausible approach than that which suggests that the choice of reference group itself produces a lowering of social horizons. There are after all a number of ways in which individuals are encouraged to tailor their expectations in line with their class position, and which are not determined by choice of reference group. The role of the educational system is especially significant in this respect.

In Britain, and in most other Western European countries, the education of the young is governed by principles of selectivity. Generally speaking, a minority are selected for intensive educational treatment in high-quality schools (public or grammar schools, *lycées*, gymnasia) while the majority are instructed in certain practical skills and elementary knowledge in less prestigious institutions (the secondary modern school and its continental equivalents). These two types of school prepare the young for entry to very different labour markets; the former leading to favourable white-collar positions or to university, and the latter to routine occupations usually of a manual kind. What is significant for the present discussion is that the two types of school serve not simply to educate the young for future positions, but also to instil into them 'appropriate' levels of aspiration and expectation. So far as the secondary modern school or its equivalent is concerned, one of its main socializing effects is to lower the ambitions of those who pass through it to accord with the opportunities in the labour market. Studies of occupational ambition among English schoolchildren have suggested that the job preferences of those in primary school are often pitched fairly high. Later, however, among those selected for secondary modern education the level of ambition drops appreciably.[12] The training and environment of this type of school appear to inculcate into children, directly or indirectly, the realization that they have been earmarked for the less desirable positions in society. Youthful high hopes they might have entertained earlier on tend not to survive the secondary modern experience. Before school-leaving age has been reached most children have begun to make 'realistic' occupational choices in place of 'fantasy' aspirations.

The experience of the minority funnelled off by grammar schools and their equivalents is markedly different. These children tend to cherish much higher hopes for the future and are altogether more optimistic about their chances of success. Indeed, there is some evidence that selection for grammar school education tends to *expand* future ambitions; this, as we might expect, is particularly true of working-class children entering grammar school.[13] These differences in level of expectation do of course correspond to very real differences in the actual market opportunities open to the two sets of school-leavers. It has thus sometimes been suggested that the secondary modern system performs a useful and humane function in psychologically preparing future members of the underclass for the harsh realities of the world awaiting them outside the school gates. However this may be, such a process also has political implications in so far as it encourages the future underclass in the art of accommodating to low status. The more successful the educational system is in doing this the more difficult becomes the task of radical groups in encouraging the disprivileged to reject their low status.

It is thus to the educational system that we must look for part of the answer to the problem of expectations. The evidence suggests that from a fairly early age low status members are *taught* to narrow their social horizons. The selection of 'appropriate' reference groups is then likely to follow as the children become adults. By this time they will have received reasonable training in the art of not 'seeing' the privileged for purposes of comparison. It would of course be an oversimplification of a complex issue to claim that the education of the future members of the underclass was explicitly designed to encourage submissive attitudes and a sense of fatalism. Formal socialization through the schools would not, in any case, usually be enough to bring about the willing acceptance of low status and rewards. As we shall argue later there is still a considerable amount of social tension at the point where new recruits take up their positions in the underclass. Again, it would probably be an exaggeration to claim that an educational system based on highly selective principles gave formal training consciously designed to induce a certain politically desirable level of expectations. At any rate it certainly is unlikely that anything of this kind would appear on the time-table of the school curriculum. Most of the social instruction bearing on this problem tends to be imparted fairly informally and unsystematically. Also, the young are themselves pretty well aware of the social status of different types of school and their relation to the occupational system. The very fact of being selected for one rather than another type of school would no doubt in itself be a powerful factor in depressing or expanding ambitions for the future. Formal advice about the limits of the opportunity structure would not then be necessary for most. In other words, the very existence of a selective educational system, having obvious and close connections with the class and occupational system, is in itself enough to foster some degree of anticipatory adjustment to future roles and rewards.

Not all industrial societies have educational systems specifically designed to fit different segments of the population into different slots in the reward hierarchy. In the United States, the early selection and preparation of the young is rejected on the grounds that it defies the canons of equal opportunity. In the American system the ethic of achievement can be more assiduously canvassed in so far as schools do not encourage the advance acceptance of 'failure' and low social status. In the absence of selective techniques the carrot of success can be dangled indiscriminately before the eyes of everyone, whatever their capabilities. One result of this is that 'fantasy' aspirations appear to be much commoner among the young in America than their English counterparts. Non-selective educational systems of the American type are probably more efficient in the use and encouragement of talent: because no one is encouraged to define himself at an early age as lacking in ability the schools can be more effective in the crucial task of motivating the young to achieve success. Innate talents are of little social use unless harnessed by the desire to develop them in socially approved directions. At the same time of course there are many casualties produced by such a system; namely, those who have been enticed by the story of success but who lack the kind of gifts needed to make it come true. The sense of failure and frustration is obviously likely to be more acute among those whose ambitions have been continuously encouraged than among those who have been mentally conditioned for low status.

British educational reforms designed to replace selective schools by a comprehensive system could, potentially, create a somewhat similar situation. When children of all levels of ability are educated together it is more difficult to prepare future recruits to menial positions for the fate awaiting them. The ideology of such a system is one designed to heighten aspirations and to inculcate the values of achievement. If this is the dominant ethos in the school it is clearly difficult to institutionalize an entirely contrary outlook in those who appear to lack the abilities which lead to success in examinations and in the market-place. Reforms in the educational system are not generally matched by corresponding changes in the occupational structure. If roughly the same proportion of young people are recruited to menial positions as before, then all that has changed in the situation of the latter is the amount of advance psychological preparation they have had. Such preparation is never completely lacking, of course. In English comprehensive schools, in particular, the system of streaming provides fairly reliable clues to enable children to work out their intended point of destination. As a number of writers have pointed out, the introduction of streaming in comprehensive schools tends to reproduce something of the former secondary modern–grammar school dichotomy under the one roof.[14] But even so, although children consigned to the bottom streams of comprehensive schools will be able to interpret the meaning of this for their future chances, they are in some ways at a disadvantage compared with those at secondary modern schools (where they would formerly have gone). In a 'stratified' comprehensive school they are bottom dogs, lacking in the qualities of academic excellence upheld by the school. Secondary modern schools, on the other hand, tend not to be stratified, and academic ability is not a basis for invidious comparison. Children in this type of school tend to single out other values for ranking purposes such as sporting ability, physical toughness, sexual knowledge, etc. And to the extent that this unofficial value system provides the academically mediocre with a moral framework in which they can seek and win acclaim, then it may be seen as a compensatory device to offset their low status in the factual hierarchy. Counter-educational ideologies of this kind are probably less easily institutionalized within a comprehensive setting. Consequently, the 'failures' may have fewer ways of preserving self-esteem.

Although it is plausible to suggest that the confrontation with the facts of inequality is liable to be more disturbing for the products of non-selective educational systems, we should be rash to predict its political implications. Even when the young have not been prepared for menial status, various responses of a non-political character seem to be more common than radical interpretations of their position. In any case, there are other agencies apart from the educational system which are responsible for raising or lowering the social horizons of the young. Family and community influences are obvious cases in point. In societies which attempt to cream off talent from the underclass, especially by way of the educational system, the family and community often play a somewhat subversive role. Characteristically, working-class parents do not foster high aspirations among their offspring, either at school or in the world of work. Unlike non-selective schools they do not encourage their young to cherish what often turn out to be false hopes about future

opportunities and rewards. There is a wellspring of social knowledge in any underclass which derives from the personal experience of low status, and which is buttressed by the knowledge
that the majority of those born into this class will remain in it.
Social advancement is not a realistic expectation for most and
the young are not house-trained to desire it. This means that
the normative system of the disprivileged tends to discourage or
prevent the upward movement of many who do in fact possess
the ability to wear, and to prosper in, a white collar. It is one of
the major dysfunctions of a stratified system that the protective
canopy put up by the underclass tends to cover all members of
the community, including those who have no need of it. Unlike
schools, members of the working class have no reliable means of
singling out potential high-fliers and socializing them differently
from those obviously destined for humbler positions. The
dampening down of aspirations to square with adult experiences
of the reward structure forms part of the social training given to
everyone. Ambition does not readily flourish in an atmosphere
thick with warnings against the danger of getting 'big ideas'. In
this way the efforts of schools to persuade talented working-class
children of the opportunities available to them are continuously
offset by disconfirming evidence provided by peers and kin. In
so far as the influences of the latter prevail, the working-class
view of limited opportunity becomes a self-fulfilling prophecy.
That is, the belief in the class system as a closed order is one of
the factors making it so. But it is important to remember that
this belief is rooted in a quite realistic assessment of the situation
as it affects the majority of working-class people; for them it *is*
a closed order. The recognition of this fact is central to our
understanding of the entire working-class value system.

But if this value system blankets the talented and untalented
young alike, how are we to explain the fact of upward mobility?
The creaming process is at least partially successful, as we know.
The answer to this question was to some extent answered earlier
in this chapter when we discussed the 'sunken middle class'. It
was then shown that successful working-class children very
often came from families which were not integrated in the life
and community of the working class, and which often held on to
a lifeline to the middle class. Children from this type of social

background would not be fully exposed to the anti-achievement values of the underclass proper. And the definitions of social reality put out by their parents would not generally run counter to the schools' own definitions. In the absence of negative attitudes towards success and opportunity the educational system has a relatively unfettered hand in the cultivation of talent, with the obvious implications for mobility we have noted.

In a way, the malfunctioning of the system for selecting and training talent, brought about by class stratification, could be said to be offset by the 'cooling out' functions which the system also performs. If everyone were fully socialized into the values of achievement and success the use of talent would be maximised; but only at the expense of creating serious frustrations among the unsuccessful. In the United States, which has gone further than any other Western society in institutionalizing the ethic of achievement, acute social tensions occur at the lower levels of the reward hierarchy. These are manifested in the exceptionally high incidence of various social phenomena, including homicide, suicide, mental illness, drug-addiction, alcoholism, juvenile delinquency, petty larceny and organized crime. Many of these phenomena have their highest incidence among the relatively disprivileged and undoubtedly reflect the serious strains attaching to low status in a society dedicated to the values of achievement and material gain. In the light of the foregoing discussion we should expect these strains to be especially acute among young recruits to low positions, since it is the young who are most exposed to the official values of achievement. In any class-stratified society there are notable tensions at the point where new members of the underclass are in the process of being fitted into their positions. As already suggested, the smoothness of this passage will to some extent depend upon the degree of advance preparation received. But even in countries like England where expectations of lower-class youth are systematically lowered, their incorporation into the social order is still quite problematic. The most publicized indication of this is the tendency towards juvenile delinquency, petty crime, vandalism, and certain kinds of gang violence among adolescent males in urban working-class communities. This type of activity occurs precisely at the stage in the life cycle when the realities of inequality are at their sharpest; namely at the point of entry to the market for manual labour. Delinquency rates tend to reach their peak round about the final year of school; in England, when the school-leaving age was raised from fourteen to fifteen years the peak age for delinquency also changed. It is true that the varied activities described by the label of delinquency are the outcome of a complex of social factors, including home and family experience, community and peer group influences, personality structure and so forth. But in acknowledging the relevance of all these factors we should not lose sight of the central point that those who typically commit acts of delinquency are part of a social category which occupies a highly sensitive place in the stratification order. It would perhaps be remarkable if those permanently selected for a life of small rewards accepted their positions with perfect equanimity. This would betoken a highly efficient system of advance socialization, which most industrial societies are not able to create, if only because of the need to celebrate the virtues of achievement. The United States has gone further than most societies in the public proclamation of these virtues. In so doing it has produced a stratification system in which low status is an especially punitive experience, and one which many people attempt to alleviate by illegal means or by symbolic attacks on the social order. As Cloward and Ohlin have suggested, it is among adolescent males that the dilemmas of low status are most acute.

It is during adolescence that decisions regarding occupational selection and routes to occupational success must be made. The adolescent male in the lower class is therefore most vulnerable to pressures toward deviance arising from the discrepancies between aspirations and opportunities for achievement . . . The 'permanent' quality of this dilemma makes it all the more acute . . . We suggest that many lower class male adolescents experience desperation born of the certainty that their position in the economic structure is relatively fixed and immutable – a desperation made all the more poignant by their exposure to a cultural ideology in which failure to orient oneself upward is regarded as a moral defect and failure to become mobile as proof of it.[15]

Although many of the activities described as deviant or delinquent may be seen as responses to the strains of low status, they are responses which entail little real challenge to the rewards structure of society. The type of 'redistribution' brought about by property thefts, and similar utilitarian forms of deviance does not affect the nature of the rules governing distribution in general. Although it is plausible to interpret adolescent vandalism, gang violence and the like as a kind of rage against the social system, it is a form of behaviour which entails the symbolic acting-out of discontent. Such behaviour is 'irrational' in the special sense of having no effect upon the conditions which produced it, and therefore serves to buttress rather than undermine the political basis of inequality.

There are of course ways of responding to the frustrations of low status which are neither political nor socially deviant, as usually understood. One of the most frequently noted of these is the acceptance of religious definitions of reality. Let us briefly examine the relationship between religion and inequality and its significance for political order.

4

In most systems of stratification religious institutions play an important stabilizing role. Among lower social strata religious beliefs are of particular significance in so far as they often present the disprivileged with an alternative system of meaning to that current in the secular world, and one in which the scale of secular priorities is dissolved or reversed. In a sense, religious institutions frequently play a similar role to revolutionary movements by attempting to bring about an alignment between the mental and material conditions of life. Revolutionary or radical movements seek to heighten the expectations of the underclass and then to adjust the material order in accordance with these expectations. Religious institutions often seek a similar kind of *rapprochement*, but by lowering the material and social desires of the underclass to conform to the existing structure of rewards. The role of religion in reconciling men to their lot by the symbolic transformation of the world has been especially crucial in traditional, pre-industrial societies. In the absence of a centralized state and the apparatus of physical coercion and control, the problem of order tends to revolve around control of the normative sphere. When all members of the society, whatever their station in life, stand under the canopy of a single faith, the divisions between strata tend to lose some of their sharper edges. But more importantly, perhaps, commitment to a single faith becomes a sophisticated means of social control, in so far as the manipulation of religious sanctions is generally the prerogative of those who support existing arrangements of power and privilege. When this faith also entails the conviction that earthly suffering is but an interlude before a heavenly reversal of fortunes, then its political implications are indeed formidable.

In industrial societies the relationship between religion and inequality is much more complex, if only because of the proliferation of different faiths and the accompanying secularization of formerly sacred spheres. The projection of expectations on to a life beyond this is less easily accomplished in societies where rational and scientific interpretations of reality increasingly hold sway. Again, the horizontal divisions of the stratification order are rarely pulled together by the vertical bonds of a common faith. In all industrial societies the attachment to the institutions and symbols of religion is decidedly greater among members of the dominant class than among members of the subordinate class. Where the latter are drawn to religion, it is often through denominations or sects which differ significantly in belief from the religious institutions of the dominant class. It seems to be that under a class system, as against a traditional status order, man's worldly interests become too sharply opposed to be reconciled on the sacred plane. Hence the stratification of the secular order is frequently mirrored, albeit very imperfectly, in the stratification of the spiritual order.

Where members of the underclass are not typically adherents of the same faith as members of the dominant class, they are not open to the same kind of normative control as are those in a 'universal' Church – for example, Catholics in medieval Europe or in modern Italy and Spain. Sects or denominations based on lower strata are in fact often hostile to the dominant Church (and sometimes to the entire social order) and so do not necessarily confer sacred approval on the rules governing inequality. It is frequently claimed, however, that they do this in an indirect, rather than a direct, way; that is, by channelling the energies of the relatively deprived into activities which cannot bring about changes in the rewards structure in their favour. The suggestion is that religious beliefs and practices of any kind enable the dis-privileged to adjust psychologically to the social punishments meted out to them. This enables running repairs to be carried out on the casualties, and potential casualties, of the class system, but does nothing to alter the system itself. Bryan Wilson, in his study of one of the Pentecostal sects, the Elimites, describes some of its social and psychological functions for those of low status.

In the assembly the believer, whatever his status outside, stands justified as a 'born-again' believer, and this primary qualification places him among the elect. Here is a circumstance in which the poorest, the most illiterate, the least socially acceptable can, theoretically, and in Elim often in practice, command a general social approval – simply by accepting Christ . . . [There is] . . . the hope of escaping the misery of life, and of the ending of the world. Such a hope is a sustaining force for those who might otherwise give up a struggle which they find is unequal to their material, social and psychological equipment. These, then, are the economically, socially and psycho-logically under-privileged – or so they might regard themselves but for the transcendent hope they find in their religious faith.[16]

It is this role of religious belief in encouraging a symbolic transformation of the world, rather than a material one, which is emphasized in the interpretation of religion as a counterweight to political radicalism. For example, a number of social historians have explained the relative political stability of English society in the nineteenth century in these terms. Halévy, Hobsbawm, and E. P. Thompson have all suggested that one important reason for the absence of revolutionary upheavals in this country, compared with other European nations, was the spread of Nonconformist religion, especially Methodism, among the English working class.[17] Had it not been for the 'counter-revolutionary' influence of the Nonconformist Churches the industrial workers, it is claimed, would probably have responded in a more radical way to the personal and social hardships of rapid industrialization. Whether Methodism did in fact play the politically stabilizing role so often assigned to it is still a matter of debate among historians. But the general problems of the relationship between religion and radicalism is one which continues to attract the attention of sociologists. Most of the studies relating to modern societies appear to favour the 'counter-revolutionary' thesis. Rydenfelt's study of communism in Sweden is a case in point.[18] His account of the opposing pull of politics and religion drew upon a comparison of two neighbouring provinces in the north of Sweden, having similarly harsh economic and physical environments. Rydenfelt found that one of the provinces gave heavy support to the Communist Party, while in the neighbouring province the Communist vote was almost non-existent. This latter province had a strong tradition of religious revivalism stretching back to the nineteenth century, and Rydenfelt suggests that the presence of established religious sects insulated workers from the appeals of communism. The difficult conditions of life in the north appeared to create a high degree of susceptibility to movements offering the promise of relief; whether men opted for the solutions proposed by political radicalism or by religious fundamentalism seems to have been a chance affair, partly dependent upon local leadership and organization. Both movements were to some extent competing for the same recruits, so that 'those workers who joined the revival movement were lost to the labour movement, and this made the socialist workers see the revivalists as political reactionaries and enemies'. [19]

Robert Blauner's account of the failure of radical labour organizations to develop among white industrial workers in the southern United States also emphasizes the counter-attractions of religion.[20] The period of rapid industrialization in the Deep South was also the period when evangelical sects flourished most profusely, partly in response to the anxieties and social dislocation which tend to accompany the abrupt shift from rural to urban industrial life. Blauner suggests that the readiness with which workers turned to religious solutions to their problems seriously undermined the basis of trade union activity and organization. He finds it 'difficult to overestimate the role of religion as a mechanism which allowed the workforce to adapt to their changed condition of life, and thus thwarted the development of movements of radical protest . . .'.[21]

It is not only historians and sociologists who have advanced the proposition that certain types of religious groups compete with political movements for the hearts and minds of the underclass. H. Richard Niebuhr, a prominent theologian, has argued a similar case. In his assessment, however, wherever religion and radical politics are in competition it is the latter which tends to be more successful because the solutions it offers are more relevant to the materially deprived.[22] Thus, far from being a counter-revolutionary force, religion is itself weakened by the greater attraction of movements designed to improve conditions in the here and now. Empirical findings on the relationship between radicalism and religion in European countries have been cited in support of Niebuhr's view. Surveys from Britain, France, and the Netherlands confirm the proposition that members of the working class are less likely to attend church or to hold religious views than are members of the dominant class, and that supporters of socialist and communist parties are more irreligious than supporters of Right-Wing and Centre parties.[23] Contrary to the 'counter-revolution' thesis, this suggests that under conditions where radical movements are already firmly implanted among the underclass religious alternatives have considerably less pull. It may well be that religious movements are more successful competitors in situations where the industrial workforce is of recent origin and where radical labour organizations would not be properly established. But this is only a hunch. In fact we know comparatively little about the general conditions which encourage lower status groups to adopt either religious or radical solutions, assuming both alternatives to be fully available. It would in any case be somewhat rash to assume that those attracted to religious movements are necessarily lost to radical politics, or even that the two kinds of activity can always be regarded as functional alternatives. Many members of the lower strata who are drawn to religion are seeking relief from the kind of personal problems which are not directly related to deprivation of a material or economic kind. Spiritual comfort and support is frequently sought by the chronically sick, the physically malformed, the bereaved, and the elderly and lonely, as well as by those suffering from various forms of emotional or mental instability. For members of lower strata who are psychically, and not simply materially, deprived religion is likely to have an especially strong appeal – and particularly those forms of belief which incorporate notions of healing by faith or which give an outlet for the uninhibited expression of emotion. Political activity could hardly be presented as a likely alternative for underclass members falling into this category. The various sects which spring up so freely among disprivileged groups appear to attract those who quite often would not be 'available' for political action, and do not recruit on any important scale from the ranks of the industrial workforce. The sects might be said to cater for the needs of those for whom the most likely alternative would be not political radicalism but personal disintegration.

Again, the view of religion as a prop to inequality and political conservatism would not accurately portray the activities of all Churches in all societies. Occasionally, the Church and its leaders have been at the spearhead of movements aimed at improving the condition of the underclass. In the southern United States, for example, political leadership among the Negro population has frequently been assumed by clergymen, and the churches have tended to provide an organizational focus for the civil rights campaign. This has been partly to do with the fact that Negro political organizations were not easily established in the repressive conditions of the southern states, so that the churches became natural rallying-points in the struggle against inequality. The evidence here suggests that religious institutions can themselves be politically radicalized under certain conditions – especially perhaps where there are no other formal political outlets for the expression of material grievances. Protestant churches have sometimes played a similar role on behalf of Africans in part of white-dominated Africa, while the Catholic Church in Eastern Europe has often been the one major focus of political opposition to communist governments.

The fact that religion and radicalism are not necessarily to be thought of as sharply antithetical is suggested by the tendency for many workers in Catholic countries, such as Italy, to be both supporters of the Communist Party and practising Christians. Christianity is open to politically radical interpretations by lower-status groups; so that even in societies dominated by a 'universal' Church the normative control of the underclass by the dominant class may to some extent be limited by systematic variations in the interpretation of religious precepts. Again, support for communism by Catholic workers suggests man's ability to compartmentalize beliefs, so that what might appear to be logical or intellectual inconsistencies in ideology are neither interpreted nor experienced as such. Given that men are capable of holding apparently contradictory beliefs and values (and perhaps only intellectuals are prone to find this troublesome), we should treat with even more caution all generalized claims concerning the political implications of religious behaviour.

Finally, it should be said that in modern industrial societies religious alternatives to political radicalism would seem to be far less significant than are various other forms of secular behaviour. Gambling, for example, provides one such form of 'release'. The social importance of gambling lies in the hope it appears to offer to the relatively disadvantaged of bringing about a dramatic improvement in their lot. In England, as no doubt elsewhere, the proportion of income allocated to betting and gaming increases with each step down the reward hierarchy, so that it is among the poorer sectors of the population that the greatest proportional outlay is made. This suggests that gambling has special significance for those who have least chance of securing high material satisfactions through occupational efforts. Persistent attempts to reverse economic fortunes through the operation of 'luck' may be partly understood as both a symptom of, and an attempt to relieve, relative deprivation. As Talcott Parsons has put it:

Gambling performs important functions for large classes in the population, very similar to those of magic, as a kind of acting out of tensions which are symbolically at least associated with the economic sphere ... [It] ... is a mechanism for expressing and thus releasing strains related to the economic context which, if this outlet were completely closed, might be diverted into other more dysfunctional channels.[24]

Undoubtedly one of the 'dysfunctional channels' Parsons has in mind is some form of opposition to the political and social order. Men who believe sufficiently in the possibilities of material redistribution through the hand of chance, may be less inclined to press for changes in the rules governing distribution. Indeed, secular beliefs of this kind may be more 'counter-revolutionary' than the appeals of religion in so far as they appear to exert a strong pull on the minds of the industrial working class. The extent to which an interpretation of the social world based on notions of chance and accident does in fact obstruct socialist or radical interpretations is an empirical question which has not been systematically investigated. All we can really say is that there seems to be a definite logical or conceptual incompatibility between the two types of outlook. But we must again bear in mind that man does have the ability to hold apparently inconsistent values and beliefs, to an extent that is often surprising to those who inhabit the world of ideas.

The interpretation of social reality in terms of chance happenings and the mysterious intervention of fate is common among groups or strata whose members have little direct control over their environment. Almost as a matter of definition, the underclass in any stratified order is much more likely to be at the receiving end of other men's decisions, than to be the originator of decisions. It is not too surprising that those who are less active than acted upon should be prone to view the social world as one governed by apparently irrational forces beyond their control. The belief in luck and its associated concepts tends to be less common among more privileged strata and those who have a more secure grip upon their social environment. Explanations of material inequality which lean on notions of chance do in a way run counter to 'official' versions of the story, by questioning the special qualities and attributes of the privileged. But it is an outlook which does not square readily with class interpretations of reality either. Class theories of inequality emphasize its systematic character and seek to locate its institutional sources. It is a perspective which above all raises the possibility of changing the reward system by human agency. Perceptions of a class kind are likely to be to some extent hindered by belief systems which stress the accidentality and fatefulness of events and their lack of responsiveness to human touch. It is this tendency for the underclass to throw up symbolic systems which explain their life situation in secular, non-political terms which is perhaps the most important of the 'safety-valves' we have discussed in this chapter. It is of course central to all discussions of class consciousness and false consciousness and their implications for political stability. In societies like our own, where serious inequalities persist, but where inequality is not morally acceptable to all, the relationship between the material sub-system and the normative order remains highly problematic. In the following chapter we examine some of these problems, and in particular those associated with the emergence of class consciousness, and the system of dominant values.

3   Class Inequality and Meaning-Systems

Sociological accounts of the normative aspects of inequality reveal the absence of any general agreement concerning the distribution of values in the class hierarchy. One school of thought maintains that the values underlying major social institutions are held in common by all social classes, though perhaps with varying degrees of commitment. A different school of thought argues that values vary sharply and systematically between classes, so that one cannot speak of a unified moral order. Engels, commenting upon the class structure of nineteenth century England, felt that the proletariat had become a 'race wholly apart' from the *bourgeoisie*. 'The workers speak other dialects, have other thoughts and ideals, other customs and moral principles, a different religion and other politics than those of the *bourgeoisie*. Thus they are two radically dissimilar nations, as unlike as difference of race could make them . . .'[1] Present day class contrasts are not normally drawn in quite such dramatic terms as this, but the 'two nations' view of the normative order continues as a powerful tradition in stratification studies. Accounts of working-class life in modern Britain often make explicit contrasts between working-class and middle-class values, so characterizing the moral order as highly differentiated.[2] This same approach is implied in the use of the term 'working-class subculture', suggesting as it does a sector of society having a distinct set of values and behavioural patterns. Similar contrasts are held to typify the normative systems of other Western societies. Hamilton suggests that in West Germany the middle and working classes 'constitute separate populations which have, for the most part, independent and relatively autonomous values.'[3] Similarly, for the United States, W. B. Miller has argued that, 'There is a substantial segment of present day American society whose way of life, values, and characteristic patterns of behaviour are the product of a *distinctive cultural system* which may be termed "lower class".'[4] Again, Hyman's much-cited paper, 'The Value Systems of Different Classes', also gives support to a class differentiated version of the normative order.[5]

The opposite approach is to emphasize the unity rather than the diversity of the general value system. The functionalist strand of thought in sociology, particularly as represented in the work of Talcott Parsons and his followers, draws heavily on the assumption of a unitary value system.[6] Merton, too, in his influential paper, 'Social Structure and Anomie', adopts a somewhat similar approach. Merton suggests that a major source of tension in modern society lies in the fact that members of the subordinate class internalize the same values as the dominant class, but lack the means for realizing them.[7] Mayer's analysis of social stratification in the United States also produces the observation that 'the working class shares a "white collar" style of life and accepts middle class values and beliefs'.[8] Contemporary political theorists have also been prone to focus on the extent of normative consensus found in the 'stable democracies'. Class variations in voting patterns and party allegiance notwithstanding, what we typically find, it is claimed, is broad agreement on values underpinning the political institutions of welfare capitalism. Thus, societies such as our own come to be labelled 'civic cultures' to distinguish them from societies characterized by sharp normative dissensus in the political sphere.[9]

The major problem raised by the class-differentiated view of the normative system is that of social control. If the subordinate class were to subscribe to a value system sharply distinguished from that of the dominant class, then the latter's normative control over the former would obviously be seriously diminished. In this situation, the dominant class would have to rely on physical coercion as a substitute for moral suasion. Thus, in societies where the use, or threatened use, of force does not appear to be the prevailing strategy of social control, we are bound to have reservations about the validity of a class-differentiated model of the moral order.

One of the main objections to the consensual model, on the other hand, is that it often fails to make clear the relationship between the normative and factual elements of stratification. Of particular relevance here is the connection between the distribution of power and the legitimation of values. All too often the assumption seems to be that common agreement on values betokens a kind of independent convergence in the moral outlook of different classes. But in fact, of course, the extent to which values are legitimized in society is largely a function of institutional power. Values are much more likely to flow in a 'downward' than an 'upward' direction; consequently, moral assumptions which originate within the subordinate class tend to win little acceptance among the dominant class. The reverse process, however, is much more marked, so that normative consensus is better understood in terms of the socialization of one class by another, rather than as independent class agreement or convergence on values.

It might be helpful if we approach this complex issue by looking at the normative order as a number of competing meaning-systems. Although there is a factual and material basis to class inequality, there is more than one way in which it can be interpreted. Facts alone do not provide meanings, and the way a person makes sense of his social world will be influenced by the nature of the meaning-systems he draws upon. So far as class stratification in Western societies is concerned it seems that we can quite usefully distinguish three major meaning-systems. Each derives from a different social source, and each promotes a different moral interpretation of class inequality. These are:

(1) The *dominant* value system, the social source of which is the major institutional order. This is a moral framework which promotes the endorsement of existing inequality; among the subordinate class this leads to a definition of the reward structure in either *deferential* or *aspirational* terms.

(2) The *subordinate* value system, the social source or generating milieu of which is the local working-class community. This is a moral framework which promotes *accommodative* responses to the facts of inequality and low status.

(3) The *radical* value system, the source of which is the mass

political party based on the working class. This is a moral framework which promotes an *oppositional* interpretation of class inequalities.

In most Western societies all three meaning-systems tend to influence the social and political perceptions of the subordinate class. Variations in the structure of attitudes of groups or individuals within this class are thus to some extent dependent upon differences in access to these meaning-systems. Any discussion of working-class values regarding the reward structure must thus concern itself both with the types of major meaning-systems 'available', and with social factors which help to account for variations in their adoption. Clearly, values are generally not imposed on men in any crudely mechanistic way. Men also impose their will by selecting, as it were, from the range of values which any complex society generates. At the same time, individuals do not construct their social worlds in terms of a wholly personal vision, and without drawing heavily upon the organizing concepts which are part of a public meaning-system. What now follows is a brief analysis of three such public meaning-systems which seem to be of major importance to the process by which men come to perceive the nature of inequality and the class structure. No claim is made that the three meaning-systems examined – the dominant, subordinate and radical – exhaust the range of normative complexity. Most societies will undoubtedly spawn a variety of subsidiary value systems which may cut across the major systems to be considered here. But given the problems and difficulties inherent in any discussion of values it seems advisable to limit the scope of the analysis to fairly broad and general categories. We begin, then, with a discussion of the dominant value system and its effect on perceptions of inequality among the subordinate class.

2

The concept of a dominant value system derives from Marx's celebrated statement that 'the ideas of the ruling class are, in every age, the ruling ideas'. This proposition rests on the plausible assumption that those groups in society which occupy positions of the greatest power and privilege will also tend to have the greatest access to the means of legitimation. That is to say, the social and political definitions of those in dominant positions tend to become objectified and enshrined in the major institutional orders, so providing the moral framework of the entire social system. It is not of course necessary to posit any monolithic social or normative unity to the groups which cluster at the apex of the dominant class. Undoubtedly they display variations in political and social outlook – as, for example, between aristocratic or traditional *élites* on the one hand and managerial or entrepreneurial *élites* on the other. However, these differences are not likely to be fundamental with regard to the values underlying class inequality and its institutional supports. With the partial exception of that group or stratum loosely defined as the intellectuals, almost all groups within the dominant class tend to define the reward system as morally just and desirable. Dominant values are in a sense a representation of the perceptions and interests of the relatively privileged; yet by virtue of the institutional backing they receive such values often form the basis of moral judgements of underprivileged groups. In a way, dominant values tend to set the standards for what is considered to be objectively 'right'. This holds not only for the rules governing the distribution of rewards but also for many other aspects of social life. In the sphere of culture, for example, the musical, literary and artistic tastes of the dominant class are accorded positive evaluation, while the typical cultural tastes and pursuits of the subordinate class are negatively evaluated. Thus in the allocation of national resources to the arts, or of honours to their practitioners, the claims of '*élite*' culture will tend to have precedence over the claims of 'mass' culture. To take a somewhat similar example, the characteristic speech-patterns and linguistic usages of the dominant class are generally regarded as 'correct', or what counts as the grammar of the language; the usages of the subordinate class are often said to be 'incorrect' or ungrammatical where they differ from the former, even though such usages may represent the statistical norm. These examples serve to illustrate that what is essentially an *evaluative* matter can be transformed into an apparently *factual* one by virtue of the legitimating powers of the dominant class. And what applies to the evaluation of linguistic forms, or of artistic tastes, applies equally to evaluations of the reward structure. Thus, to accept Marx's proposition regarding the genesis of 'ruling ideas' is not to subscribe to a conspiracy theory of society; it is rather to acknowledge that moral and political rules hold sway not because they are self-evidently 'right', but because they are made to seem so by those who wield institutional power.

Now the more completely the subordinate class comes to endorse and internalize the dominant value system, the less serious will be the conflicts over existing inequalities. There is of course a good deal of variation in the extent to which lower strata come to accept the version of social reality held by upper strata. The caste system of traditional India provides an extreme case of a stratified order permeated throughout by values legitimizing the power and privilege of dominant groups. The subordinate class in industrial society does not generally subscribe so completely to a meaning-system which confirms its own inferiority. Nevertheless, certain tendencies in this direction are observable. Studies by McKenzie and Silver, and Eric Nordlinger have demonstrated that large segments of the British working class express moral commitment to many of the dominant class symbols and institutions which sanction inequality. Furthermore, there appears to be fairly widespread disapproval among the subordinate class for bodies such as trade unions which attempt to redress the balance of advantages in their favour.[10]

This phenomenon of a class, or at least a large segment of it, endorsing a moral order which legitimizes its own political, material, and social subordination is open to somewhat different assessments. On the one hand, it can be taken as evidence of a socially desirable political consensus – a social order free from disruptive class conflicts. Or, on the other hand, it can be understood as an example of a society in which the dominant class has been especially successful in imposing its own definitions of reality on less privileged groups. Thus, to equate political and social consensus with the good society, as so many contemporary writers do, is really to state a concealed preference for a system in which the dominant class has effectively translated its own values into a factual moral order binding on all. From this point of view, societies such as France or Italy, where the dominant class has been less successful in shaping the workers' perceptions, are regarded as somewhat inferior political species.[11] Unlike the 'stable democracies' or the 'civic cultures' the subordinate class in France and Italy is prone to *incivisme*: that is, it puts a different interpretation upon inequality, and its own place in the social order, from that provided by the meaning-system of the dominant class. Thus, from the consensualist standpoint, a class-conscious proletariat is regarded as dysfunctional for the political system, in so far as it is less amenable to normative control by the dominant class than is a deferential proletariat.

Deferential interpretations of the reward and status hierarchy stem from acceptance of the dominant value system by members of the subordinate class. It should be emphasized here that deference as a general mode of understanding and responding to the facts of low status does not necessarily entail a sense of self-abnegation. Rather, it tends to be bound up with a view of the social order as an organic entity in which each individual has a proper part to play, however humble. Inequality is seen as inevitable as well as just, some men being inherently fitted for positions of power and privilege. To acknowledge the superiority of such people is not to demean or belittle oneself, since all must benefit from their stewardship of society. In their discussion of working-class Conservatives, McKenzie and Silver point out that:

. . . deferentials, although seeing themselves as subordinate, do not feel themselves inferior. English deferentials feel themselves the moral, if not the social, equals of the elite because they appear to accept the classic doctrine that all who properly fulfil their stations in life contribute worthily to the common good . . . English working class deferentials are provided with a sense of esteem by the very ideas which justify and explain their social and political subordination.[12]

Acceptance of the dominant value system by members of the subordinate class does not necessarily promote deferential orientations. Equally consistent with such acceptance is a view of the reward structure which emphasizes the opportunities for self-advancement and social promotion. This aspirational model of reality endorses the class and status system as it stands, but also represents it as a relatively open order in which men of talent and ability can, with effort, rise above their present station. Thus, whereas the deferential version of the social world accepts the class system as a fixed, unchanging order, the aspirational version allows for the social exchange of personnel between classes, while accepting the necessity for classes as such.

Both deferential and aspirational models are extracted from the dominant value – or meaning-system; but whether one rather than the other is accepted as a workable moral framework seems, to some extent at least, to be related to structural variations within the subordinate class. There are, for example, various indications that deferential attitudes tend to be most marked among groups and individuals who directly experience the social influences and judgements of dominant class members. Included among these might be those whose occupations bring them into immediate face-to-face contact with employers; or those who live in rural communities and small towns with established local status systems. Under such conditions, nationally derived symbols of class and status are reinforced by becoming 'operationalized', as it were, through personal contact and regular social encounters with high-ranking members of the community. As Lockwood puts it:

Local status systems, therefore, operate to give the individual a very definite sense of position in a hierarchy of prestige, in which each 'knows his place' and recognizes the status prerogatives of those above and below him. For the deferential traditionalist, such a system of status has the function of placing his work orientations in a wider social context. The persons who exercise authority over him at his place of work may not be the same persons who stand at the apex of the local status system, but the structural principles of the two social orders are homological; and from neither set of relationships does he learn to question the appropriateness of his exchange of deference for paternalism.[13]

Aspirational interpretations of the reward structure appear to flourish among those in a quite different social situation. We should, perhaps, expect such an outlook to be found most commonly among members of the working class who are downwardly mobile. Those who have had some experience of white-collar styles of life have access to a window on the social world which is closed to most of their class peers. Hence their symbolic meaning-system is likely to incorporate many of the elements common to the dominant class, while also differing sharply from the deferential view, which draws essentially upon the experience of *inherited* subordinate status. In addition to the downwardly mobile, it could be expected that those whose occupations make them somewhat marginal to the working class would also be prone to visualize the reward system as a fairly open opportunity structure. Those in positions such as foreman, policeman, supervisor, etc., are in the anomalous situation of exercising authority over members of the subordinate class without actually being part of the dominant class. There is not much reliable evidence concerning the general outlook and attitudes of those who are 'in' but not altogether 'of' the subordinate class; but we might speculate that working-class authority figures would, by virtue of their position, be committed to dominant values, but not to a deferential interpretation of them. As mentioned in the previous chapter, there are some indications that marginal members of the subordinate class are relatively successful in encouraging educational ambition and performances in their children. And this might be taken as one index of a general aspirational outlook similar to that held by the downwardly mobile. However, given the absence of information on this score we cannot get much beyond plausible hunches. Even less appears to be known about the extent to which Western societies vary among themselves in the distribution of deferential and aspirational norms. British society, for example, is said to be especially productive of deference, while in the United States aspirational values are said to be far more entrenched.[14] If this is in fact so, then it is clear that the interpretation of any given society's dominant value system is not simply a function of variations in the social location and attributes of different groups. Obviously, if American or Australian workers who are in face-to-face relations with their employers, or who live in small communities, do *not* tend towards a deferential outlook, then we cannot posit a general connection between images of society and structural factors. The stock of class symbols 'available' in a society must to some extent be influenced by specific historical and cultural factors; consequently, we should expect to find variations in the dominant value systems of different societies, and therefore certain variations in the meanings given to inequality, structural similarities notwithstanding.

3

The *subordinate* value system; the generating milieu of this meaning-system is the local working-class community. There is an abundance of studies of the patterns of attitudes and beliefs typifying what is sometimes called the working-class or lower-class subculture.[15] In so far as it is possible to characterize a complex set of normative arrangements by a single term, the subordinate value system could be said to be essentially *accommodative;* that is to say its representation of the class structure and inequality emphasizes various modes of adaptation, rather than either full endorsement of, or opposition to, the *status quo*. Hoggart portrays this underlying theme of the subordinate value system as follows:

When people feel that they cannot do much about the main elements in their situation, feel it not necessarily with despair or disappointment or resentment but simply as a fact of life, they adopt attitudes towards that situation which allow them to have a liveable life under its shadow, a life without a constant and pressing sense of the larger situation. The attitudes remove the main elements in the situation to the realm of natural laws . . .[16]

The subordinate value system tends to promote a version of the social order neither in terms of an open opportunity structure nor as an organic unity; rather, strong emphasis is given to social divisions and social conflict, as embodied in the conceptual categories of 'them' and 'us'. This power or conflict model of the reward structure is clearly different from any which could be derived from outright endorsement of the dominant value system. Indeed, it is a general perspective which casts some doubt on the morality of the distributive system and the persistent inequities it generates. At the same time, however, it would be misleading to construe the subordinate value system as an example of normative opposition to the dominant order. Least of all, perhaps, should it be understood as exemplifying class-consciousness or political radicalism. Some writers have tended to overemphasize the political significance of the power or conflict model, and to see it as evidence for a highly differentiated normative system. Dahrendorf, for example, has leaned heavily on working-class notions of 'them' and 'us' to support a general theory of class conflict.[17] More recently, Newton's study of the social bases of the British Communist Party claims that there are 'elements in the British working-class culture which can be tapped by the BCP. Outstanding among these is the *powerful class consciousness* which is to be found in almost any working-class community.'[18] Again, 'At the purely local political level, class-conscious "them" and "us" awareness is expressed in the strong community spirit which is remarked on by almost every writer on working-class communities. The CP is fairly successful where it can draw on this expression of class consciousness . . . .'[19]

This is a fairly common interpretation of the political significance of the subordinate value system, or what most writers refer to as the 'working-class subculture'. But if we examine its content at all closely we are bound to be rather sceptical of such politicized constructions. To begin with, Hoggart's catalogue of working-class usages (which is the main empirical source of the power model so far as England is concerned) refers primarily to the experience of authority relations with such diverse figures as policemen, civil servants, local government officials, and petty bureaucrats, as well as with employers. Now resentment at bureaucratic officialdom is certainly likely to be more sharply felt among the subordinate than the dominant class. But this is hardly to be equated with political class consciousness in the usual meaning of that term. Nor, again, is the pervasive sense of communal solidarity which is typically found in the underclass milieu to be equated with a class outlook on politics and society. As Hoggart himself points out, the communal or solidaristic aspect of working-class life is largely confined to *interpersonal* relationships, and for 'most people it does not develop into a conscious sense of being part of the "working class movement" '.[20] Conventionally, to describe workers as class conscious is to refer to their commitment to a radical or oppositional view of the reward structure of capitalist society. Typically, of course, this type of outlook is associated with Marxist or socialist movements, and does not emerge of its own accord from the under-class milieu. Indeed, it could be said that the subordinate value system represents something of a bulwark to political class consciousness, in so far as it entails adaptive rather than opposi-tional responses to the *status quo*. As Westergaard has argued, the solidarities of class and the solidarities of community are antithetical rather than complementary.[21] Subordinate class communities throw up their distinctive value systems more or less independently of one another; there is no 'national' subor-dinate value system in the way that there is a truly national or societal dominant value system. The similarity in the normative patterns of working-class communities derives largely from the similarity of the conditions they are exposed to. They generate a meaning-system which is of purely parochial significance, repre-senting a design for living based upon localized social knowledge and face-to-face relationships. A class outlook, on the other hand, is rooted in a perception of the social order that stretches far beyond the frontiers of community. It entails a macro-social view of the reward structure and some understanding of the *systematic* nature of inequality. In a way, becoming class con-scious, at least in the ideal-typical sense, could be likened to learning a foreign language: that is, it presents men with a new vocabulary and a new set of concepts which permit a different translation of the meaning of inequality from that encouraged by the conventional vocabulary of society. In some social settings, and for many individuals, becoming class conscious must often amount to what is virtually a normative transformation; at any rate, it draws upon a meaning-system which is far removed from that embodying accommodative or adaptive responses to the facts of subordinate status.

In certain respects, accommodation to material insecurity or deprivation betokens a kind of fatalistic pessimism. Hoggart catalogues some of the many working-class expressions indicating the necessity for making mental adjustments to material hard-ship: 'What is to be will be'; 'that's just the way things are'; 'grin and bear it'; 'y've got to tek life as it comes'; 'it's no good moaning'; 'mek the best of it . . . stick it . . . soldier on . . .' etc., etc.[22] Although fatalism and the reluctant acceptance of one's lot is a prominent theme of the subordinate value system, it is by no means the only major response compatible with adaptation. A no less important element in the accommodative outlook is the 'instrumental collectivism' typified by the trade union movement. Trade unionism is one of the few forms of socio-political organization which is indigenous to the subordinate class, and yet based upon society rather than community. And, in so far as men combine in the attempt to improve their material situation they could not be said to have a purely fatalistic outlook; commitment to trade unionism implies a belief that conditions should and can be improved, which is quite different from the pessimistic resignation enshrined in the popular sayings quoted above. However, the fact that unionism is closely geared to the moral framework of the subordinate value system is reflected in the movement's aims regarding the distribution of rewards. Collective bargaining and its attendant strategies imply a general acceptance of the rules governing distribution. Organised labour directs its main efforts towards winning a greater share of resources for its members – not by challenging the existing framework of rules but by working within this framework.

In this respect it is reasonable to regard trade unionism and instrumental collectivism generally as an accommodative response to inequality. Collective bargaining does not call into question the values underlying the existing reward structure, nor does it pose any threat to the institutions which support this structure. Trade unionism could in fact be said to stabilize the modern capitalist order by legitimizing further the rules and procedures which govern the allocation of resources. At least, the fact that many modern capitalist states give legal protection to trade unions, and social honours to their leaders, suggests that the strategies of collective bargaining do not cause serious inroads to be made into the privileges of the dominant class. It was of course on these grounds that Lenin, among others, contrasted 'trade union consciousness' with 'class consciousness', arguing that only the development of the latter could lead to genuine social and political transformation.[23]

Trade union consciousness, as one of the emergent properties of the subordinate value system, exemplifies what is perhaps the defining characteristic of this meaning-system; namely, its uneasy compromise between rejection and full endorsement of the dominant order. Put in rather broad terms, it could in fact be suggested that the subordinate value system represents what could be called a 'negotiated version' of the dominant value system. That is to say, dominant values are not so much rejected or opposed as modified by the subordinate class as a result of their social circumstances and restricted opportunities. Members of the underclass are continually exposed to the influence of dominant values by way of the educational system, newspapers, radio and television, and the like. By virtue of the powerful institutional backing they receive these values are not readily negated by those lacking other sources of knowledge and information. However, since such values are the moral representation of the interests and opportunities of more privileged groups, their 'appropriateness' as far as the less privileged are concerned is problematic. The tendency among the under-privileged is not to reject these values, and thus create an entirely different normative system, but to negotiate or modify them in the light of their own existential conditions. This principle of negotiating the dominant value system in response to the pressures of underclass life is similar to what Rodman has referred to as the 'lower class value stretch'.

By the value stretch I mean that the lower class person, without abandoning the general values of the society, develops an alternative set of values . . .
Lower class persons in close interaction with each other and faced with similar problems do not long maintain a strong commitment to middle class values that they cannot attain, and they do not continue to respond to others in a rewarding or punishing way simply on the basis of whether these others are living up to the middle class values. In this way they need not be continually frustrated by their failure to live up to unattainable values. The resultant is a stretched value system with a low degree of commitment to all the values within the range, including the dominant middle class values. This is what I suggest as the major lower class value change, rather than a change in which the middle class values are abandoned or flouted.[24]

Rodman's formulation draws attention to the fact that the subordinate class has two distinct levels of normative reference; the dominant value system and a 'stretched' or 'negotiated' version of it. We can perhaps add to this formulation by suggesting, further, that which of the two frames of reference is actually drawn upon will be situationally determined; more specifically, it could be hypothesized that in situations where purely abstract evaluations are called for, the dominant value system will provide the moral frame of reference; but in concrete social situations involving choice and action, the negotiated version – or the subordinate value system – will provide the moral framework. It may be useful to give one or two examples in illustration of this distinction.

Values associated with occupational success and material achievement are an important element in the normative system of the dominant class. As far as the subordinate class is concerned, there seems to be some evidence that achievement values are similarly endorsed in some abstract sense, but not as guides to action in existential situations. Thus, when working-class youths are asked to specify which occupations they would like to enter if they had a completely free and Utopian choice, they frequently mention positions which rank high on the scale of material reward and social honour.[25] In other words, their 'fantasy' aspirations tend to reflect the influence of the dominant, achievement values. Their 'realistic' expectations, however, are far more modest and tend to be based on the social knowledge of restricted opportunities: that is, in situationally defined contexts the subordinate value system will be more likely to provide the appropriate frame of reference.

To take a somewhat similar example, it is a common finding of social research that industrial workers often endorse middle-class criticisms of the trade unions when asked to express an opinion. Cannon reports that only 33 per cent of a sample of skilled workers disagreed with the view that the trade unions have too much power.[26] A 1969 survey found that 67 per cent of trade union respondents agreed with the statement that their leaders' activities constituted a 'threat to the prosperity of the country'.[27] At the same time, however, there is little evidence that workers are opposed to trade union action in furtherance of their own particular demands, whatever they may say in answer to questions about trade unionism in general. Attitudes tapped by opinion polls or by interviews are likely to reflect the influence of the dominant value system, since generally the questions do not specify precise situational contexts. But day-to-day experiences at the workplace are likely to be more decisive in shaping a man's views of collective bargaining and strike activity than are the abstract moral precepts of the dominant value system.

One final illustration of this normative ambivalence will suffice. This concerns popular evaluation of the occupational status order. It was noted in Chapter I that members of the subordinate class tend to acknowledge the status superiority of dominant class positions, and the status inferiority of subordinate class positions. It is this apparent lack of sharp disagreement between classes in the evaluation of prestige which has encouraged many sociologists to speak of a consensual status order. However, it is equally well established that those who rank low in this 'factual' status order are also prone to elevate their *own particular occupation* to a higher social level than it publicly enjoys; and this they do while acknowledging the subordinate status of manual work *in general*.[28] In other words, when asked to evaluate positions as an abstract moral exercise, the dominant value system furnishes the primary frame of reference; but when required to evaluate their own individual social worth, by assessing their own specific occupations, members of the subordinate class are much less securely bound by the moral criteria of the dominant class. Thus there is not necessarily a logical inconsistency in the fact that subordinate class members demote the social value of manual work while at the same time excluding their own particular manual occupations from this blanket evaluation.

All this serves to highlight the significant fact that the norms underlying many aspects of subordinate class behaviour do not come to be objectified into a positively sanctioned and overarching moral system. Subordinate values cannot be transformed into an objectivated moral system because the generating milieu of these values is typically the local underclass community; and this simply lacks the institutional power to legitimize a normative system which is sharply at odds with the dominant value system. Consequently, members of the subordinate class are constrained to accept the dominant moral framework as an abstract and perhaps somewhat idealized version of reality, although their life conditions tend to weaken its binding force in the actual conduct of affairs. It is from this tension between an abstract moral order and the situational constraints of low status that the subordinate value system emerges. It is a system of meaning which cannot oppose the orthodoxies of the dominant class, although it may neutralize them to some extent. On these grounds, it is useful to regard subordinate values as a negotiated form of dominant values, rather than as a completely differentiated normative construct.

The fact that the subordinate class tends to have two levels of normative reference, the abstract and the situational, is highly relevant to the problem posed at the beginning of this chapter: namely, whether it is more plausible to speak of a common value system shared by all classes, or a class differentiated value system. To some extent the answer will depend on the level of generality at which the inquiry is pitched. Thus, studies of working-class attitudes which rely on questions posed in general and non-situational terms are likely to produce findings which emphasize class consensus on values; this is because the dominant value system will tend to provide the moral frame of reference. Conversely, studies which specify particular social contexts of belief and action, or which rely on actual behavioural indices, are likely to find more evidence for a class differentiated value system; this is because in situational contexts of choice and action, the subordinate value system will tend to provide the moral frame of reference. It should of course be said that members of any social class are often likely to distinguish between abstract values and concrete situations. But the reason why such a distinction is particularly crucial to our understanding of subordinate class behaviour is that the moral standards and evaluations which make up the abstract framework originate within another, more powerful, social class. Members of the dominant class, on the other hand, do not take their abstract standards from a different social class, and are therefore likely to experience less serious discrepancies between institutionalized values and situational acts. Thus it is not a simple distinction between concreteness and generality which is at issue here, but also the relationship between class power and the moral framework of inequality.

It is clear from the foregoing discussion that the conditions which favour the emergence and acceptance of the subordinate meaning-system are those associated with the growth of metropolitan areas of high population density. Engels, writing of conditions in nineteenth century England, noted the role of cities and large towns in loosening the normative bonds between *bourgeoisie* and proletariat.

> If the centralisation of population stimulates and develops the property-holding class, it forces the development of the workers yet more rapidly. The workers begin to feel as a class, as a whole . . . [Thus] . . . their separation from the bourgeoisie, the development of views peculiar to the workers and corresponding to their position in life, is fostered, the consciousness of oppression awakens, and the workers attain social and political importance . . . Without the great cities and their forcing influence upon the popular intelligence, the working class would be far less advanced than it is.[29]

Engels similarly noted that paternalistic relations between workers and their employers were greatly undermined by the development of mass manufacturing processes and large-scale industry. Only when the 'sentimental bond between them . . . had wholly fallen away, then only did the worker begin to recognize his own interests and develop independently; then only did he cease to be the slave of the bourgeoisie in his thoughts, feelings, and the expression of his will. And to this end manufacture on a grand scale and in great cities has most largely contributed.'[30] The heavy concentration of underclass populations in homogeneous communities could be said to produce a certain 'moral density' necessary for the development of a subordinate value system. However, it should again be emphasized that this type of social setting does not generate political opposition to the dominant order. Oppositional values are the creation of political agencies based on society rather than on community and are not derivative from the subordinate value system. So let us now consider the role of such political agencies, and more specifically the mass radical party, in shaping man's perceptions of class and inequality.

The *radical* value system; the social source of this meaning-system is the mass political party based on the subordinate class. The party's interpretation of the reward structure draws upon a set of precepts – typically of a socialist or Marxist variety – which are fundamentally opposed to those underlying the institutions of capitalism. It thus promotes a view of the social order which is quite unlike that which finds expression in instrumental collectivism or trade union consciousness. The radical value system purports to demonstrate the systematic nature of class inequality, and attempts to reveal a connectedness between man's personal fate and the wider political order. In order that the sometimes obscure link between cause and effect may be made manifest, a new set of political concepts and symbols is introduced. Thus, the subordinate value system restricts man's consciousness to the immediacy of a *localized* setting; and the dominant value system encourages consciousness of a *national* identity; but the radical value system promotes the consciousness of *class*. European socialist movements based on an egalitarian ideology, and having their own distinct traditions, heroes, songs, slogans, and political imagery, have created a composite political culture in which class perceptions and evaluations occupy a central place. This type of class-oriented meaning-system is an important counterweight to that of the dominant order not only in an obvious political sense, but also at an individual level. That is, attachment to the ideals of socialism can provide men with a sense of personal dignity and moral worth which is denied them by the dominant value system. Judged by the standards of the dominant class, manual workers' contributions to society are not highly regarded, and they rank relatively low in the scale of social honour. The radical value system, on the other hand, affirms the dignity of labour and accords the worker a position of honour in the hierarchy of esteem. Members of the subordinate class who endorse radical values are thus provided not merely with a certain explanatory framework for the interpretation of social facts, but also with a more favourable social identity. Oscar Lewis has suggested that where socialism becomes the dominant ideology of the society it may have a positive effect on the morale of those formerly regarded as the subordinate class. This was indicated by his study of a poor community in Cuba, before and after the Revolution. Lewis found that in the post-revolutionary situation:

The physical aspect of the slum had changed very little, except for a beautiful new nursery school. It was clear that the people were still desperately poor, but I found much less of the despair, apathy and hopelessness which are so diagnostic of urban slums in the culture of poverty. They expressed great confidence in their leaders and hope for a better life in the future. The slum itself was now highly organized, with block committees, educational committees, party committees. The people had a new sense of power and importance. They were armed and were given a doctrine which glorified the lower class as the hope of humanity.[31]

So far as Western capitalist societies are concerned, there seems to be a considerable range of variation in the extent to which radical values are disseminated among the subordinate class. The United States, for example, is one of the few industrial societies lacking a mass working-class party; and partly as a result of this, radical or class interpretations of inequality are not an important element in the normative make-up of that society. In France and Italy, on the other hand, political class consciousness is much more marked, partly because the mass working-class parties in these countries continue to espouse radical doctrines. Elsewhere in Europe, and particularly where Social Democrats form the mass working-class party, there seems to have been a long-term trend towards de-radicalization. Although at present it is only possible to speculate on the outcome of this trend, it seems quite likely that it could have a decisive effect on the political perceptions of the subordinate class. It seems plausible to suggest that if socialist parties ceased to present a radical, class-oriented meaning-system to their supporters, then such an outlook would not persist of its own accord among the subordinate class. Once the mass party of the underclass comes to endorse fully the values and institutions of the dominant class, there remain no major sources of political knowledge and information which would enable the subordinate class to make sense of their situation in radical terms.

This is really to assert that the mass party has a potentially more formative influence on the political perceptions and understanding of the subordinate class than is generally acknowledged. All too frequently it is assumed that the party's doctrines on issues related to inequality are in some sense an expression of its supporters' evaluations of these issues. Thus, a decline in the party's radicalism tends to be explained as the outcome of changing attitudes among its supporters, to which the party must respond. However, this approach may overestimate the extent to which political perceptions are formed *independently* of the party. Once established among the subordinate class, the radical mass party is able to provide its supporters with political cues, signals, and information of a very different kind from those made available by the dominant culture. To a considerable degree workers may look to their party for political guidance in the attempt to make sense of their social world. They themselves have relatively little access to knowledge, so that the political cues provided by their own mass party are of key importance to their general perception of events and issues. As Philip Converse has pointed out:

Unless an issue directly concerns . . . [uneducated lower strata] . . . in an obviously rewarding or punishing way . . . they lack the contextual grasp of the system to recognize how they should respond to it without being told by elites *who hold their confidence* . . . If a communication gets through and they absorb it, they are most willing to behave 'ideologically' in ways that will further the interests of their group.[32]

To see the party simply as a receptacle for the political views of its supporters is really to underestimate its potential influence in shaping the social consciousness of the subordinate class and in providing its members with a distinctive moral framework for interpreting social reality. If, as so many observers suggest, there has occurred a marked decline in working-class radicalism in the post-war period, this may be due at least as much to changes in the nature of the party as to changes among its supporters. Some of the factors associated with de-radicalization are examined in the next chapter; but what is of immediate relevance here is the possible long-term effect this may have on the normative aspects of stratification.

It was suggested at the beginning of this chapter that one way of conceiving the normative side of inequality was in terms of a number of different meaning-systems. Three such meaning-systems – the dominant, subordinate, and radical – were held to be of special significance in understanding the attitudes and responses to inequality on the part of the subordinate class. These three systems of meaning, each presenting social reality in a different light, are all to be found within the subordinate class in varying degrees. Put in metaphorical terms, the overall meaning-system of the subordinate class could be likened to a kind of 'reservoir' fed by three major 'normative streams', each flowing from a different 'institutional source'. Attitudes towards the social order held by any given members of this class would be likely to reflect the influences of this normative mix, rather than the kind or rigorous intellectual consistency which would be produced through exposure to only one major meaning-system. At the same time, we should expect to find patterned variations in a man's social outlook to be associated with differences in the degree of his exposure to the three meaning-systems in question. The implication of all this is that the general structure of attitudes towards inequality is likely to undergo a significant change if the radical value system should cease to be part of the overall normative complex. In terms of our metaphor, the reservoir of meaning would be seriously diluted if the normative stream represented by the radical value system should run dry at its source – namely, the mass working-class party.

One likely consequence of such an occurrence is that the subordinate value system would increasingly provide the framework of social meaning among the working class. That is, interpretations of, and responses to, class inequalities would probably be weighted more heavily in the direction of adaptation and accommodation. The realities of class would continue to be highly salient to man's construction of his social world; but the responses to these realities would be bounded by the moral categories of the underclass community and the instrumental collectivism of the trade union movement. This would promote an image of the reward structure in terms of a division between 'them' and 'us', in which certain limited gains could be made through bargaining techniques; but it would not promote an alternative moral view of society nor principled opposition to the subordinate status of the working class.

To accept the possibility that socialist parties might cease to be a major source of radical values is certainly not to claim that such values would then be expunged from the political culture. It seems altogether likely that they would continue to influence the outlook of certain groups, such as intellectuals and students, as well as small parties on the political fringe. But the decisive question here is the strength of the social links between these groups, the intellectuals in particular, and the subordinate class. Historically, of course, the system of values we call socialism was developed mainly by western intellectuals who then disseminated it among the industrial workers. As Kautsky pointed out in a celebrated passage:

The vehicle of science is not the proletariat, but the *bourgeois intelligentsia*: it was in the minds of individual members of this stratum that modern Socialism originated, and it was they who communicated it to the more intellectually developed proletarians who, in their turn introduce it into the proletarian class struggle where conditions allow that to be done. Thus, socialist consciousness is something introduced into the proletarian class struggle from without and not something that arose within it spontaneously.[33]

If the radical value system continued to flourish among the intellectuals, they could, it might be argued, repeat the same task of political indoctrination described by Kautsky. However, it is important to bear in mind that intellectuals tend not to be successful in influencing workers unless there are strong institutional links between them. In nineteenth-century Europe those links were provided by the mass party. It was through the medium of the party that the radical intelligentsia were able to broadcast the ideas of socialism and so exert a powerful influence on the outlook of the industrial working class. In western societies today, however, radical intellectuals do not have the same degree of access to socialist parties; consequently there are now few, if any, institutional links between the socialist intelligentsia and the workers, so that the former's political influence on the latter is minimal. The de-radicalization of the party typically leaves the radical intellectuals politically isolated, as exemplified by the case of the New Left in various western societies. Intellectuals, or students, may attempt to forge independent links with workers, but these tend to be fragile and short-lived. It would seem that the mass party is one of the very few social agencies which has the potential to condition the outlook of the working class in a radical direction. If, for whatever reason, it chooses not to utilize this potential, then we might expect a gradual de-radicalization of the working class to set in.

De-radicalization is not of course to be equated with the acceptance or moral endorsement of existing inequality. Resentments over the distribution of rewards are likely to persist, even in the midst of affluence. What this could mean is that the tensions generated by inequality would be directed into non-political channels. In particular, certain forms of 'subcultural deviance' might be expected to flourish more readily among groups which are both relatively deprived and de-politicized. Apolitical 'deviance' would perhaps be most likely to occur among those members of the subordinate class who fall outside the orbit of the organized labour movement. Unionized workers are able to accommodate themselves to the reward system through the collective bargaining process; and, as the American experience shows, this process is not impaired by the absence of a mass radical party or class ideology. But for those numerous groups which lack access to formal bargaining agencies, personal adjustment to the facts of low status may be somewhat more problematic.

Obviously, the political relevance of working-class parties is not confined to their educative or normative functions. Quite apart from their potential influence on the meaning-system of the subordinate class, socialist parties are commonly committed to the re-distribution of material and social rewards. The next two chapters take up this theme by examining the impact on the reward structure of working-class political parties which have assumed the mantle of power. Chapter 4 considers the role of Social Democratic governments in western capitalist societies, and Chapter 5 examines the impact of Communist governments in Eastern Europe. Although those who wield political power are able to affect men's lives in ways not directly related to the problem of inequality, it is only this particular problem which will concern us in the following pages.

4   Inequality and Political Ideology:
Social Democracy in Capitalist Societies

In all industrial societies political movements have emerged with the express aim of changing the reward structure to the advantage of the working class. With the partial exception of the United States, the creation of an industrial workforce has everywhere brought in its wake the creation of socialist or communist parties committed to changing the existing arrangements of power and privilege, whether by revolutionary or constitutional means. It is well known, however, that the history of European socialist parties is a chronicle of the gradual and continuous dilution of these early radical aims. The constitutional changes which have occurred in working-class parties, and the Social Democratic parties in particular, have everywhere reflected the same trend: the early abandonment of revolutionary tactics, followed by the slow erosion or traditional socialist doctrines concerning the distribution of rewards along egalitarian lines. But, despite this long-term process of de-radicalization, it would be incorrect to say that ideological differences on the problem of inequality no longer exist between socialist and *bourgeois* parties in capitalist societies. The former parties still derive their mass support from members of the subordinate class, and it is to the material and social improvement of this section of society that socialist parties are still nominally committed. To deny this would be to claim that the tensions brought about by the stratification system no longer find their expression through political institutions. More, it diverts attention from the nature of the ideological transformation which underclass parties have undergone in the present century. The first question to be asked is, in what way does socialist ideology at the present time constitute a challenge to the reward system of modern capitalism? The answer to this may help us to a fuller understanding of the complex relationship between European social democracy and class inequality.

The problem of socialist ideology is posed in its most acute form when working-class parties assume political power in capitalist societies. Governments in modern highly centralized states have the power to effect fundamental changes in the stratification system. Consequently, when the state is controlled by political representatives of the underclass it may be assumed that social and material advantages will be redistributed on a somewhat more equal basis than when the party of the dominant class is in power. This at any rate is the major assumption underlying the theory that elections in Western society represent a form of 'democratic class conflict'.

[In] all countries the more deprived strata, in income and status terms, continue to express their resentments against the stratification system or perhaps simply their desire to be represented by politicians who will seek to further redistribute the goods of society, by voting for parties which stand for an increase in welfare state measures and for state intervention in the economy to prevent unemployment and increase their income *vis-à-vis* the more privileged strata.[1]

In this view, the 'shape' of the stratification system is seen to be open to manipulation by political agencies. If socialist parties or governments were openly *not* committed to a redistribution of resources in favour of the less privileged the moral content of modern electoral politics, and perhaps much of its present class basis, would quickly evaporate. Against this view, however, it has been argued that political ideology can have no significant or lasting effect on the stratification system of industrial society. It is suggested that the 'needs' or 'demands' of a modern technological order give rise to a certain type of social structure, irrespective of government philosophies.[2] According to one variant of this view, the existing structure of inequalities has important functions for the motivation and recruitment of men to different social positions in the most efficient manner. Any tampering with this, because of a doctrinal commitment to egalitarianism, or on similar grounds, is likely to run counter to the innate 'logic' of modern industrialism. The political colouring of governments is thus seen to be more or less irrelevant to the structure of inequality. Marxist critics of social democracy have advanced a somewhat similar proposition, though of course on very different grounds. They have argued that Labour governments cannot radically improve the position of the subordinate class because they are tolerated in power only in so far as they refrain from making serious inroads into the privileges of the dominant class. Indeed, it is sometimes further argued that certain sections of the dominant class may often welcome the temporary advent of a socialist administration because labour leaders are uniquely placed to control working-class demands for a greater share of society's resources.

In opposition to these views, Social Democrats claim that left-wing governments have consistently introduced legislation designed to improve the lot of the less privileged. By initiating reforms in taxation and education, by the expansion of health and welfare programmes, full employment policies and the like, the position of the working class and the poor has been significantly improved under Labour regimes. Even when the means of production are largely in private hands, and where the economy is still organized along market principles, a government with a democratic socialist ideology, it is suggested, is still able to some extent to shift the balance of advantages in an egalitarian direction.

These opposing claims concerning the impact of socialist governments on the reward structure of capitalist society have generally been conducted in polemical terms. But, although this is an issue which inevitably arouses passions, we need to adopt a fairly agnostic approach to the problem if we are to reach any satisfactory conclusions. One way we might put the matter to the test is by comparing the stratification systems of Western countries which have had stable social democratic governments with those which have not. Historically, Labour or Social Democratic parties in Europe have for the most part assumed the role of the main opposition party in Parliament. Government by the Right or Centre has been far more common than government by the Left, even in the present century. The major exceptions to this tendency are the parties of the Scandinavian countries and, to a lesser extent, Britain. The Social Democratic Party in Sweden has had a virtual monopoly of political power since the early 1930s. The Norwegian Labour Party has been in office, almost without interruption, for the past thirty years or more. The Danish Social Democratic Party has been the largest party in the country since 1924, when it formed its first government; for most of the time since then the Social Democrats have been the leading political force, ruling either alone or in coalition. The British Labour Party cannot match this kind of performance; but nevertheless it has occupied the seat of power for considerably longer than most European parties of the Left. It has now been in office for about half the post-war period, no doubt long enough to have made its impact felt on the reward structure. If, then, we wished to test propositions concerning the relationship between inequality and socialist ideology it would be reasonable to compare Britain and the Scandinavian countries with the rest of Western Europe. One slight complication here is the fact that in several European countries in the post-war period socialists have been invited to join Conservative-dominated governments, as junior coalition partners. However, in this situation there appear to be too many political constraints to enable the socialists to translate their ideology into legislation. As Miliband has put it, 'social-democratic ministers have generally been able to achieve little inside these hybrid formations. Far from presenting a threat to the established order, their main function has been to contain their own parties and to persuade them to accept the essentially conservative policies which they themselves have sanctioned. For the most part, participation on this basis has been a trap not a springboard.'[3] It is likely that any attempt to make inroads into the privileges of the dominant class would meet with some resistance; but this resistance is clearly more difficult to mobilize against a majority socialist government, especially one of long standing, than against junior coalition partners. Consequently, the political distinction made above should still hold good.

To answer in a definitive way the question of how far, if at all, Labour governments succeed in altering the balance of class advantages would of course require a major comparative study. All that can be attempted here is a brief review of some of the available evidence which has a direct bearing on the problem. It should be made clear that what is here at issue is not whether the 'Social Democratic' countries exhibit radically different stratification orders from their European neighbours, since this is patently not the case. Rather, it is whether they show the kind of *variations* on the overall European pattern which could plausibly be attributed to differences in government ideology.

2

One useful measure of the class distribution of advantages and life-chances is that provided by social mobility rates. Variations in the degree of social exchange between the classes illustrate national differences in the extent to which privileges are inherited from one generation to the next. The extent of downward mobility in a society is generally regarded as a more telling index of its openness than the rate of upward mobility. High upward mobility can often be attributed to the expansion of white-collar and professional positions and would not necessarily indicate any erosion of inherited privilege. A high rate of downward mobility, on the other hand, is a sign that white-collar groups are being displaced, even though the actual degree of social demotion may not usually be very great. Lipset and Bendix, in their comparison of mobility rates for advanced Western countries, suggested that the amount of social exchange between classes was fairly uniform in industrial societies.[4] This finding was commonly used to support the argument that stratification systems are shaped by the technological and industrial 'base' of society, and are not susceptible to ideological manipulation. S. M. Miller's more comprehensive analysis of mobility rates has, however, pointed up certain significant variations in the pattern of social exchange for countries at a roughly similar level of industrial development.[5] Of particular interest in the present discussion is Miller's construction of an 'index of inequality'. This is a measure of the opportunity for sons of white-collar families to remain in the same social class as their parents, as compared with the opportunities for the sons of manual workers to move up into white-collar positions. The following table shows variations in the degree of openness in Western European countries. The first column shows the degree of white-collar self-recruitment, and the second column shows the degree of upward movement from the manual working class. Column three expresses these two measures as an index of inequality; the lower the figure in this column the greater the degree of openness in the class system.

TABLE 4.1 *Social self-recruitment and upward mobility*

	(1) *Non-manual into non-manual* %	(2) *Manual into non-manual* %	(3) *Index of openness* ($\frac{1}{2}$) %
Great Britain	57·9	24·8	234
Denmark	63·2	24·1	262
Sweden	72·3	25·5	284
Norway	71·4	23·2	308
France	79·5	30·1	264
Netherlands	56·8	19·6	290
Belgium	96·6	30·9	313
West Germany	71·0	20·0	355
Italy	63·5	8·5	747

Source: S. M. Miller, op. cit.

These differences are not particularly marked; and in view of the notorious problems associated with the collection and comparability of mobility data the figures must be interpreted with a good deal of caution. With this caveat in mind, it will be observed from the above table that Britain and the Scandinavian countries rank relatively high in the scale of openness. Interestingly enough, Svalastoga, using somewhat different measures from Miller, produced broadly similar results.[6] Svalastoga found that the countries which scored highest on an index of political egalitarianism (defined in terms of Left-Wing voting strength) also scored highest on the index of social mobility. Of the six European countries in the survey, Sweden, Denmark, and Britain were shown to have a greater degree of political egalitarianism and of social class exchange than France, West Germany, and the Netherlands. These findings must be interpreted with the same caution as those in Miller's survey. The two sets of results do not tally exactly, but there is sufficient agreement in their general pattern to warrant a certain amount of confidence in them. At any rate, to express it in the most guarded manner possible, if all disbelief about the comparability of mobility data were temporarily suspended, the evidence would seem to favour those who wished to show some connection between political ideology and social stratification.

This raises the problem of the manner by which socialist governments are able to improve the opportunity structure of the underclass. There are a number of different ways by which the advantages of low status groups can be increased so that they are in a better position to make inroads on the traditional privileges of high status groups. One way of doing this is by bringing about changes in the system of education. In modern societies the possession of educational certificates plays an increasingly important part in determining an individual's placement in the reward structure. A person's 'investment' in his own education is one of the most profitable forms of investment he can now make, as measured by the returns on his 'capital' throughout his working life. Consequently, the educational system is a powerful mechanism for altering the balance of advantages between classes, and as such it is inevitably the focus of much political conflict. The educational system is also particularly suitable as an instrument of social change in so far as, in most countries, it is directly under the control of the state. Unlike many other aspects of a reward system governed by market forces it is, therefore, immediately responsive to political decrees. Thus, if we are concerned with exploring the relationship between stratification and ideology, national variations in the structure of educational opportunity should be a source of enlightenment.

Of particular interest here are differences in the pattern of recruitment to higher education, in so far as universities and colleges are the main avenues to *élite* positions. In broad terms, the relationship between class structure and higher education is similar in all Western European countries; the middle and upper classes everywhere furnish the great majority of the student population, with recruits from working-class homes being in a distinct minority. However, within this overall pattern there are certain variations relevant to the problem under review. Table 4.2 shows the percentage of the university student population of working-class origin in various European countries.

TABLE 4.2 *Percentage of university students of working-class origin in European countries circa 1960*

	%		%
Great Britain	25	France	8
Norway	25	Austria	8
Sweden	16	Netherlands	5
Denmark	10	West Germany	5

Sources: O.E.C.D.;[7] Dahrendorf;[8] Tomasson; Scase.[9]

Although in none of these countries does working-class representation in the university come anywhere near to mirroring the proportion of working-class people in society, it is noticeable that under-representation is considerably less marked in Britain and Scandinavia. In these countries the proportion of working-class students never falls below 10 per cent; elsewhere, the figure never reaches 10 per cent. In the case of Britain, however, the relatively high proportion of manual workers' children at university is not a recent phenomenon, but was also a feature of the pre-war period. It is thus not attributable to the impact of socialist administration. The most that could be said in this respect is that given the tendency for the working class to decline in size relative to the middle class, the long-term stability in the percentage share of the working class amounts to a small overall gain in university representation. The introduction by the post-war Labour government of a system of maintenance grants may have been a significant factor in keeping working-class representation up to its pre-war level. The intensified demand for higher education at the present time might otherwise have given a greater edge to those with the ability to pay. In Scandinavian countries, too, the government has provided financial help for needy students by offering long-term loans at low interest rates. It seems unlikely that financial provisions of this type would not be one important factor accounting for the class variations in student populations. Norway and Sweden differ from England in that these two countries have shown a gradual increase in the working-class share of university places in the post-war period. Tomasson reports that in Norway, children of manual workers made up only 11·8 per cent of the student population in the period 1930–39. Following the post-war educational reforms this proportion was steadily increased, reaching 25 per cent by the early 1960s. Similarly, in Sweden, students of working-class origin accounted for only 8 per cent of university enrolment in 1947; this increased to 12 per cent in 1953, to 14 per cent in 1960, and to 16 per cent in 1963. This upward trend is expected to continue as a result of the recent reorganization of secondary education.[10] In these two countries, at least, then, it seems quite reasonable to speak of a gradual improvement in the opportunity structure of the subordinate class brought about by direct political agency.

The proportion of working-class youths in the full-time student population is perhaps the best single index of the openness of the educational system as a whole. This is because at all educational levels the selection process tends to cut into the numbers of working-class children more severely than into the numbers of middle-class children. As a result, the proportion of the former potentially available for higher education gets progressively smaller as each hurdle is crossed. Thus, the class composition of the university population is to some extent, though not wholly, dependent on differential rates of class 'survival' in secondary schools. In most European countries secondary education is based on selective principles, a system which tends to reinforce the pattern of class advantages. Entry to grammar or public schools, *lycées*, gymnasia, and the like, is generally available for only a minority of children, the majority going on to lower-status schools in preparation for routine or manual occupations. Comparative data on the class composition of the grammar school and its continental equivalent are rather meagre, but there are reliable figures for England, Sweden, France, West Germany, and the Netherlands. These are given in Table 4.3, shown on page 112.

Again, we find that working-class children are more strongly represented in selective schools in England and Sweden than elsewhere. It is likely that the Swedish figures underestimate the overall percentage of working-class children in selective schools since they are based on students in higher gymnasia. The comparatively high proportion of working-class grammar school children in England and Wales is no doubt partly to do with the existence of a well developed system of private education. The fact that many wealthy middle-class parents prefer to send their children to public schools means that competition for grammar

TABLE 4.3 *Percentage of grammar school children of working-class origin circa 1960*

	%		%
Great Britain	52	Netherlands	19·5
Sweden	23	France	17·0
		West Germany	16·0

Source : O.E.C.D.[11]

school places is to some extent lessened. But even so, this would not altogether account for the differences in class composition of English selective schools and those on the Continent. It should, of course, be borne in mind that although working-class children may be well represented at the point of entry to grammar school, they have much higher attrition rates than have middle-class entrants. Little and Westergaard have shown that in England and Wales 36 per cent of all working-class children born in the late 1930s entered grammar school at the age of eleven; but only 9·5 per cent were still there at the age of seventeen.[12] Comparative data on early leaving are not available but it might well be that countries which practise a more stringent selection of working-class children may also have a higher retention rate. If this were so, national differences in the class composition of *upper* levels of selective schools would be narrower than those shown in the above table. However, it seems unlikely that the differences would evaporate completely, on the grounds already stated; namely, that higher working-class representation at university probably denotes a higher working-class representation in the sixth form of selective schools.

But whatever the comparative advantages in secondary education available to the working class in England, we cannot explain them as an outcome of socialist government policies. This is because roughly the same opportunity structure has existed since about 1910. A more obvious link between the educational system and socialist ideology is the attempt by Labour and Social Democratic governments to replace selective schooling by a 'comprehensive' system. This has proceeded further in Britain and the Scandinavian countries than elsewhere in Europe. The advocates of comprehensive education tend to see it a means of overcoming the influences of social class on the academic performances of the young. By abolishing early selection and the physical segregation of children into different types of school, environmental disadvantages can be effectively countered. Strongest resistance to the comprehensive principle has tended to come from those who see it as a threat to traditional middle-class privileges in education, and for whom the abolition of selection raises the spectre of a universal 'levelling down' and the lowering of traditional standards. The debate over educational reform has thus been a political debate over the redistribution of class advantages. And where Social Democrats have been in power they have acted more decisively in favour of bringing such changes about than have their *bourgeois* opponents.

At the same time, it should be pointed out that the extent to which comprehensive schooling does in fact confer advantages on working-class children is by no means a settled issue. Some studies have suggested that in schools in which streaming is practised the conditions of selective education are reimposed under the comprehensive roof.[13] Where this is the case, the political goal of educational reform may be very largely thwarted. According to Tomasson, the switch to comprehensive education in Sweden and Norway has been carried through *without* the retention of selectivity or streaming principles. Thus, 'Among western European nations only Sweden and Norway . . . can be regarded as having done away with this most basic structural support of a class-linked educational system.'[14] It is clearly of some significance that the European countries with the strongest tradition of socialist government have moved nearest to the type of educational system which appears to offer, in theory at least, greater advantages to children of the subordinate class. School reforms occurring in these countries may of course be linked to changes in the industrial and occupational structure. The more technologically sophisticated a society becomes, the greater the need for a labour force rich in skills and education. But this is not a sufficient explanation if only because other Western European nations are undergoing similar changes without necessarily opting for similar reforms. As Dixon has pointed out, '. . . the reforms in the educational systems of Scandinavian countries arise from clearly held social and political philosophies of the Social Democratic or Labour parties in those countries . . .' [15] and cannot be explained simply as a response to the 'needs' of modern industry.

All this does suggest that governments ideologically committed to improving the position of the underclass can bring about certain changes in the overall balance of rewards and opportunities. The variations are not particularly great and not all of them (especially in the case of Britain) could be attributed to the impact of socialist ideals. Nevertheless, the variations all appear to be in the direction necessary to give some mild support to the claim for an independent 'ideological effect'. Of course, differences in opportunity structure associated with education and social mobility are not necessarily related to differences in other aspects of the reward structure. A central tenet of the socialist movement has been the commitment to egalitarianism, understood as the levelling of material rewards accruing to different social groups or classes. We must therefore also consider the extent to which countries with socialist governments differ on this dimension of inequality from their Western neighbours.

3

Traditionally, the Labour movement has been associated with attempts to equalize income distribution through such measures as taxation and the provision of state welfare. In Britain, the introduction of a national system of social and welfare services was regarded as one of the most distinctive achievements of the post-war Labour government. The Scandinavian Social Democracies, too, are commonly held up as models by the most enthusiastic advocates of social welfare and security. The provision of state welfare is reasonably interpreted as an egalitarian measure in so far as its intention generally is to give social and material benefits to those who lack the resources to pay for them. If the cost of providing these services is disproportionately met by wealthier groups, then this represents an effective form of redistribution. Similar ends can be achieved by progressive taxation on income, death duties, wealth taxes, and the like. By these and other means it is administratively possible for egalitarian-minded governments to tilt the balance or rewards in favour of the subordinate class, within the framework of a market economy.

These are the common strategies adopted by socialist governments in capitalist societies. But whether or how far they have been successful in making inroads upon inequality is a matter of some dispute. Some writers have suggested that a market system has an irresistible pull towards inequality; socialist governments may attempt to curb these tendencies, but they simply reappear in new forms. A market system guarantees the economic and social power of the middle class, and this cannot seriously be eroded by government decrees. Against this, however, a number of economists have suggested that action by the state can have, and has had, a marked effect on income distribution. It has, in particular, been claimed that a considerable levelling out of incomes occurred in Britain during the period of the post-war Labour government, as compared with the pre-war years. Socialist policies were certainly viewed with considerable alarm by large sections of the middle class, as longstanding differentials between white-collar and blue-collar incomes began to be eroded. The 'crisis of the middle class' under a Labour government was a prominent topic of political debate in Parliament and the Press. The reasons for middle-class anxiety were spelled out by the *Economist* in its review of income trends during the first two years of Labour rule. It pointed out that the average real income of the manual worker had increased by between 10 and 35 per cent over the pre-war level; the average white-collar salary, in contrast, had fallen by between 20 to 30 per cent over the same period. Income from property and investments had fallen even more sharply.

At least 10 per cent of the national consuming power has been forcefully transferred from the middle classes and the rich to the wage earners. A gradual approach towards greater equality of income is an ideal that appeals to many people even among those classes who would suffer from it. But there has been nothing gradual about this transfer. There has been no attempt to analyse the consequences of such a sudden wrenching of the social mechanism, with all that it implies in the removal of incentives to effort and ambition. There has been no attempt even to discuss the question whether it is right that a war in which all classes contributed what they could should leave behind it, as an accidental by-product, a social revolution of these dimensions. There has been no attempt to base the changes on the merits of those who have gained or on the demerits of those who have lost; the sentimental assumption has simply been made that anybody who is paid by the week is always noble and right, while anyone who is paid by the month is inevitably an exploiter.[16]

A number of studies appeared in the early 1950s which gave statistical support to the proposition that there had been a distinct levelling off in incomes under the Labour administration. In the 1960s, however, the validity of this proposition was questioned by Titmuss, among others, who argued that data on income tax returns gave a misleading picture of income distribution, and probably exaggerated the extent to which levelling had occurred.[17] The issue remains a hotly controversial one, partly because of its political implications and partly because of the methodological problems raised in measuring income trends. Most authorities in this field would probably accept that *some* equalization has in fact occurred, if only on a fairly modest scale. But whether this is to be attributed to the policies of a socialist government, or to factors unrelated to political ideology is something we must examine. It has been suggested, for example, that the tendency towards income narrowing is a common or universal feature of advanced industrialization. A variety of social and economic factors are held to account for this process. One of the most important is the expansion of education and the general spread of skills throughout the population. Universal literacy and the extension of basic schooling has meant a steady increase in the numbers available for skilled positions, thereby reducing the market advantages of these positions, relative to those requiring little or no skill. The gradual reduction in the income differential between routine white-collar work and manual work is one well-documented instance of this trend. Another is the narrowing gap between skilled and unskilled manual incomes. Secondly, there has been a long-run tendency for the share of total income accruing to labour (wages and salaries) to increase, and for the share accruing to property to decrease. Income from property tends to be much more unevenly distributed than income from employment; so that a relative decline in the share of the former is a factor making for greater overall equality. Thus, for Britain, Feinstein has shown that the proportion of national income accruing to property has been halved in the last fifty years or so.[18] It could not of course be claimed that this expansion in labour's share is the outcome of socialist ideology. Much of it is accounted for by the increase in the size of the workforce, especially the white-collar section, and by the decline in the number of self-employed and small family businesses.

The pressures making for income equalization are thus seen to be related more to long-term industrial and social trends than to egalitarian political philosophy. Some social theorists have been sufficiently impressed by these trends to posit an irreversible relationship between advanced industrialism and increasing income equality. However, recent data on occupational incomes in Western Europe throw considerable doubt on this proposition. Table 4.4 provides comparative figures on income differentials for various European countries and the United States. The figures refer to average male earnings of manual and non-manual occupational groups, expressed as multiples of the earnings of unskilled labourers. In the light of the present discussion, three points are of immediate interest.

Firstly, there is considerable variation in income ranges between societies in the advanced industrial fold. The 'logic' of industrialism does not seem to have produced a corresponding logic of income differentials.

Secondly, variations in the degree of equalization do not

TABLE 4.4 *Average earnings by occupational groups in selected Western countries*
(Expressed as multiples of average earnings of male unskilled labourers)

	United Kingdom			Sweden			Norway			Denmark
	1935	1955	1960	1953	1957	1963	1956	1960	1964	1965
Unskilled manual	1·00	1·00	1·00	1·00	1·00	1·00	1·00	1·00	1·00	1·00
Skilled manual	1·51	1·43	1·49	...	...	...	1·14	1·14	1·15	1·24
Clerks	1·50	1·20	1·30	1·30	1·30	1·30	1·00	1·10	1·00	1·30
Lower admin. and professional staff	2·40	1·40	1·60	1·50	1·70	1·80	1·20	1·30	1·30	2·10
Higher admin. and professional staff	3·80	3·40	3·50	2·00	2·90	3·10	2·20	2·40	2·40	4·30

	France			West Germany			United States			Italy
	1956	1962	1964	1957	1961	1965	1939	1950	1959	
Unskilled manual	1·00	1·00	1·00	1·00	1·00	1·00	1·00	1·00	1·00	1·00
Skilled manual	1·38	1·42	1·46	1·26	1·24	1·25	1·50	1·48	1·57	1·24
Clerks	1·40	1·60	1·50		1·00	1·00	2·10	1·60	1·80	1·50
Lower admin. and professional staff	2·40	2·70	2·80	1·50	1·50	1·40	...	...	...	2·00
Higher admin. and professional staff	4·90	5·40	5·50	2·10	2·00	1·80	3·20	2·30	2·40	7·00

Source: United Nations, *Economic Survey of Europe in 1965*, Part II, Table 5.16

appear to be related to variations in government ideology. Thus, although differentials between unskilled workers and high rank-ing white-collar professionals are lower in Norway than in most other countries; this is not true of Sweden and Denmark. Indeed the latter two Social Democracies have wider differentials than both the United States and West Germany.

Thirdly, in a number of countries, including Britain and Sweden, there was a slight *increase* in class differentials in the 1960s. There appears to be no clear sign of an inexorable trend towards wage equalization.

It should be borne in mind that these figures refer to average earnings within broad occupational categories, and that the dispersion of *individual* incomes within these categories is bound to be wider than that shown in the Table. Clearly, in most of these countries large numbers of top professional and managerial staff will earn considerably more than two or three times the wage of an unskilled worker. In addition, high ranking white-collar staff can often expect to supplement their incomes with perks of various kinds. But if these things hold equally for all industrial societies this should not invalidate the comparisons between them.

The distribution of occupational income gives us perhaps the best overall view of the reward structure, because for the great majority of the population the main or only source of income is from employment. However, the income profile can of course be significantly altered by the system of taxation. In fact all West European countries operate highly progressive tax systems, so that the disproportionate share accruing to top income groups is partially offset by steep taxes. The *Economic Survey of Europe in 1965* reported that in countries for which data were available there had been a marked trend towards easing the burden of taxation on the richest stratum (the top income tenth) so that the proportion borne by lower income groups had increased.[19] Thus, in Norway the richest income tenth paid 40 per cent of the total income tax in 1957; in 1963 they paid just over 35 per cent. The tax burden on the bottom 5 income tenths increased from 17 per cent to 19·1 per cent of the total. In Britain, tax relief for the wealthiest income group has been considerably greater than this. The top income tenth paid 73·2 per cent of the tax bill in 1954; 10 years later they were paying 59·5 per cent. (Figures for Sweden were not available, but the *Survey* reports that the Swedish tax system, like the Norwegian, is less steeply progressive than the British system.)

More recent evidence for Britain has been provided by Hughes. He points out that between 1964 and 1967 various changes occurred in the weighting of different groups of taxes, the overall effect of which was distinctly regressive.[20] For pensioner households and those at the very lowest income levels no adverse changes have been registered, but for most working-class families the proportion of income retained after tax has shown a definite decline, after allowing for all benefits. Hughes suggests that some of this shift towards increasing inequality had occurred before the 1964 Labour government had taken office (and this is confirmed by the *Survey* referred to above) but that much of it is attributable to the policies of the new government. He concludes that, under the Labour administration, the evidence is 'overwhelmingly that although some measures have aided particular low-income groups, the main drive of the system towards inequality has in fact been heavily reinforced'.[21] It is no doubt significant, too, that the middle class appears to have expressed considerable optimism about its economic position under the 1964 Labour administration. Lewis and Maude, in their 1969 study, found that 'more of the middle classes think their standards have risen faster in relation to other people's than think they have risen more slowly'. In the upper middle class alone, the figures were 36 per cent and 22 per cent respectively, while at lower levels there was more optimism still.[22] As the authors themselves point out, this indicates a striking change of attitude from that current among white-collar groups in the immediate post-war years. And the evidence on class differentials cited above would appear to make middle-class optimism, even under a Labour government, well justified.

Thus, if the first post-war decade was a period characterized by a certain degree of income equalization, the second decade was one in which this trend went into reverse. This appears to have been a general West European pattern, and one which has not been noticeably checked by Social Democratic administra-

tions. Speculation concerning the drive towards income equalization seems to have been greatly influenced by the conditions of
the early post-war period. But the recent concern with the extent
of poverty in affluent societies marks a distinct change in mood,
and underlines the point that the drive towards inequality, inherent in a market system, is not easily held in check.

4

All this must raise serious doubts on claims concerning the
ability of parties or governments based on the underclass to
redistribute material rewards in an egalitarian manner. After
thirty-five years of socialist rule in Sweden, income differentials
between working-class and middle-class occupational groups are
no narrower than in Western societies ruled by *bourgeois* governments. Only in Norway, a largely rural, sparsely populated
country has Social Democracy left a distinct imprint on the
distributive system. In Britain, the advent of the 1945 Labour
government coincided with the general egalitarian and welfare
trends which were common to almost all West European countries during the period of post-war reconstruction. Labour's
return to power in the mid-1960s coincided with the general
reversal of these trends. This does not offer much support to the
view that socialist governments in capitalist societies can combat
the pressures of the market more effectively than can their opponents. Where income narrowing has occurred this has been
due more to long-run social and industrial trends than to the
effect of egalitarian ideologies.

Thus, in so far as countries with a record of socialist rule
could be said to differ from others in the pattern of rewards, it
is in the relative openness of their class systems, as indicated by
rates of mobility and educational opportunities. In other words,
Social Democrats appear to have been more able or willing to
broaden the social base of recruitment to privileged positions
than to equalize rewards attached to different positions. Reform
of the educational system along comprehensive lines is one of the
strategies adopted by socialist governments towards this goal. It
is still too early to measure the effectiveness of this particular

strategy, but it is important to acknowledge the *intention* behind it, since it does mark a crucial difference in political ideology between socialist and conservative groups. If the structure of opportunities is radically changed, so that large proportions of the underclass move into privileged positions, while those in the dominant class suffer demotion, this can be said to be a change in the stratification order. That is, it is theoretically possible to keep a system of hierarchic positions intact, while drastically altering the pattern of recruitment to them. Governments committed to improving the lot of the subordinate class may thus attempt to achieve this end by changing the structure of opportunities but not the differentials in reward. Thus, the resistance to educational reforms by members of the dominant class may be understood as an attempt to prevent the erosion of longstanding inherited privileges and the social continuity of the class structure.

Social Democratic emphasis on changing the reward structure by creating greater opportunities for the underclass stems from what might be termed the 'meritocratic' interpretation of socialism. That is, inequality is understood as lack of 'fairness' in the competition for well rewarded positions; socialist reform should therefore be designed to put the race for privileges on a more equitable footing. The meritocratic interpretation of socialism presents a view of the social order which is sharply at odds with the traditional conservative view. C. A. R. Crosland, one of its most eloquent advocates, expresses its political implications as follows.

The essential thing is that every citizen should have an equal chance – that is his basic democratic right; but provided the start is fair, let there be the maximum scope for individual self-advancement. There would then be nothing improper in either a high continuous status ladder . . . or even a distinct class stratification . . . since opportunities for attaining the highest status or the topmost stratum would be genuinely equal. Indeed the continuous traffic up and down would inevitably make society more mobile and dynamic, and so less class-bound.

Conservatives like to claim that this is the doctrine of modern Tory radicalism . . . [but] . . . I do not believe that such a society in any way resembles the true ideal of most Conservatives. Consider its most obvious implications – completely free, competitive entry into industry; an end to all nepotism and favouritism; a diminution, if not the virtual elimination, of inheritance . . . and generally the extrusion of all hereditary influences in our society – and contrast these with actual Conservative policies in these various spheres, and with their emotional attachment to precisely the most traditional and hereditary features of British life.[23]

The meritocratic interpretation of socialism thus presents a definite challenge to inherited class and privileges. But while it differs from Conservative ideology it differs as much, if not more, from the 'egalitarian' interpretation of socialism. In this latter view, socialism is concerned with eradicating privileges, not with changing the principles by which they are allocated. Rich and poor would still exist in a meritocracy because rewards would still be determined by occupational functions and market skills. Egalitarian socialism, on the other hand, denies the relevance of the market as a distributive mechanism; differences in reward can only be justified by differences in social need, not by economic power. Moreover, the status and power of the industrial working class is to be enhanced not by providing greater opportunities for personal advancement, but by giving workers parity with white-collar personnel in the decision-making process at the workplace. Under meritocratic socialism, classlessness would be produced by continuous, large-scale social exchange of personnel from one generation to the next. Under egalitarian socialism, classlessness would be produced by the distribution of reward on the basis of need and by the substitution of 'industrial democracy' for traditional authority structures.

These two interpretations are clearly incompatible, but both are intertwined in the complex of socialist doctrines and teachings concerning the reward system of industrial society. It would be true to say that the egalitarian view is the more radical of the two in so far as it embodies principles which are opposed to the present system based on private ownership of productive property and a free market economy. The meritocratic interpretation, on the other hand, is perfectly compatible with a modern capitalist order. Indeed, its emphasis on the most efficient use of talent would in many ways make a positive contribution to such an order. Opposition to meritocratic principles is likely to come mainly from traditional elements in the society – aristocratic, or landowning or military groups, and the like. But those sectors of the dominant class whose fortunes are most closely bound up with modern industry are likely to be somewhat less hostile. In the United States, where traditional elements are comparatively weak, meritocratic ideals are widely accepted by the dominant class. This fact by itself suggests how readily an 'equality of opportunity' version of socialism can be accommodated to the institutions and values of modern capitalism. Indeed, it has led at least one observer to suggest that socialist parties have never flourished in America because the basic values of that society are already socialist in character.[24] Needless to say it was not the egalitarian view of socialism that this observer had in mind.

So far as European Social Democratic parties are concerned, it would seem that the emphasis on egalitarianism has increasingly declined in favour of the meritocratic view. This is suggested not only by post-war revisions of party constitutions and policies, but also by the material on inequality presented above. This does not necessarily mean that socialist parties or governments no longer differ in their attitudes to inequality from *bourgeois* parties or governments; on the whole they still do, despite popular polemics to the contrary. But the meritocratic view is reasonably interpreted as a de-radicalized form of socialism, in that it constitutes much less of a challenge to the institutional order of modern capitalism than do egalitarian measures aimed at dismantling private property and the market system.

The kind of egalitarian measures which Social Democratic governments are likely to favour are those related to the provision of welfare and social services. Although the concern for welfare is generally understood as an important element in socialist doctrine, it is again pertinent to note that it is easily accommodated into the framework of the existing moral order. As many observers have noted, the provision of welfare in modern capitalist societies can be accounted for on a number of grounds unrelated to egalitarianism. It has been suggested, for example, that the allocation of benefits to the less privileged serves to damp down radical or revolutionary movements. In this view, the relatively low costs incurred by the dominant class in the provision of welfare is more than offset by the prevention of a more drastic kind of redistribution. The introduction of social security legislation by Bismarck, for example, was a quite explicit attempt to undermine the growing appeal of Marxian socialism among the German working class. Secondly, it can plausibly be argued that welfare provisions are acceptable to the dominant class, or many influential sections within it, because they result in increased efficiency. Workers who enjoy good health, housing, and basic education are more productive than workers who live in squalor, ignorance, and disease. The gain to the dominant class which results from increased output more than compensates for the outlay on welfare. Thirdly, it has been suggested that the payment for, and use of, social services does not necessarily produce a net advantage for the subordinate class. Social security contributions in most welfare states tend to be either regressive, by requiring a flat rate payment, or proportional to income. The effect of this is to impose a relatively greater burden on lower-income groups than does direct taxation. It seems to be the case that much of the redistribution which does take place is of a 'horizontal' rather than a 'vertical' kind. That is, it is contributions from groups like the young or the unmarried which are largely subsidizing payments to the sick or the elderly or those with large families. It is in other words, a form of 'life cycle' transfer, which does not necessarily entail much movement of resources from one *social class* to another. In some ways, welfare provisions appear even to favour more privileged groups. Retirement pensions, for example, tend to confer advantages on those who live longest; since white-collar professionals have greater life expectations than manual workers they will take a disproportionate share of the benefit fund to which all have contributed. Class differences in the use of collectively financed educational facilities provide an even more obvious case of a net advantage accruing to white-collar groups. As Professor Glenn has pointed out, the 'initiation and extension of Social Security may actually be in the interests of the more privileged classes . . .'

The upper classes may support Social Security because it in effect forces the lower classes to help bear the costs of their own old age, disability and unemployment and because it tends to lessen political pressure for genuine interclass transfers of wealth to provide for the basic needs of indigents.

Many people at intermediate income levels support or acquiesce to extension of Social Security because they are willing to forgo some income during the more prosperous stages of the life cycle in return for an increment of income at a time when money has greater marginal utility. Consequently one does not necessarily have to invoke altruism, egalitarian values or even effective political pressure from the lower classes to explain Social Security and the income redistribution that results from it.[25]

Bearing all this in mind, it seems unlikely that the commitment to welfare can be explained in terms of any single political or social motive. Clearly, a whole array of factors is involved; political prudency, a concern with the efficient use of manpower, the modesty of the distribution actually effected, the social benefits provided to middle income groups, as well as moral or political sympathy for the underclass. What does seem certain is that the advent of the welfare state cannot simply be put down to the victory of egalitarian or socialist principles. In Lord Beveridge's view, 'Social Security is not a political question at all. It is neither Socialist nor Capitalist. It is simply common sense.'[26] This view is perhaps supported by comparative data on welfare expenditures. As Table 4.5 shows, Western European countries dominated by Right or Centre governments in the post-war period do not necessarily allocate a smaller share of their national resources to welfare than do countries which have governments of the Left.

TABLE 4.5 *Welfare expenditures in West European countries*

(Percentage of G.N.P. allocated to Social Security expenditure in 1960)

Sweden	12·4	West Germany	16·1
Denmark	11·1	Belgium	14·2
Great Britain	11·0	Austria	14·0
Norway	10·3	France	14·9
		Switzerland	7·7

Source: Cutright.[27]

It could reasonably be argued, of course, that it is among the socialists that the most vigorous champions of welfare have generally been found. Social Democratic governments have also met with some opposition from certain middle class interest groups when introducing health and housing and similar welfare reforms. Nevertheless we should not lose sight of the fact that the attempt to remedy inequality by the welfare approach brings about relatively little disturbance of the stratification system. As a result it is much more palatable to the dominant class than certain other solutions would be.

The reasons why socialists advance proposals for dealing with inequality are no doubt very different from the reasons which make such proposals acceptable to the dominant class. For socialists, the attack on inequality contained in educational reforms or welfare measures springs from an ideological commitment to improve the lot of the underclass. But their eventual acceptance by the dominant political class rests on quite different grounds. Without too much exaggeration we could in fact say that whether or not socialist approaches to inequality become politically acceptable depends on whether or not they confer advantages on the dominant class, or at least an important section of it. Welfare and meritocratic reforms do carry such advantages on the grounds already stated. Egalitarian reforms designed to change the rules of distribution and ownership do not. It is not particularly surprising, then, that the former interpretation of socialism is accepted as politically legitimate, while the latter is regarded as 'irresponsible' or 'Utopian'. Those who make judgements about the victory of socialist ideals, even on the minds of Conservative or *bourgeois* governments, generally fail to make it clear that it is only the former version of socialism they are referring to. It is this former version, too, which now very largely represents the official ideology of Social Democratic or Labour parties in Europe. Viewed historically, this amounts to a major trasformation in the moral and political outlook of the socialist movement, or at least its leading political and parliamentary bodies. Socialist parties were initially committed to abolishing the system of ownership and rewards of capitalist society and replacing it with a system based on egalitarian principles. All the major Social Democratic parties in Western Europe have now abandoned this aim. This process of de-radicalization has occurred over an extensive period of time, but in most cases the final break with traditional or egalitarian socialist doctrines occurred in the

1950s, coinciding with first European taste of affluence. One implication of this is that wherever Social Democrats form the main party of the subordinate class there is no major political force in society which represents a radical challenge to the reward system of modern capitalism. It is thus of some importance to consider the factors which promote or encourage the gradual de-radicalization of the underclass party. This chapter thus concludes with a brief discussion of some of the factors underlying the transformation of Social Democratic ideology.

5

One common explanation for the waning radicalism of socialist parties is that which traces its source to changes in the social and economic condition of the proletariat. Developments in party attitudes to inequality, at least in the period following the Second World War, have been seen to be related to overall improvements in the material conditions of life. It is suggested that whereas unemployment and low wages are conducive to working-class radicalism, economic security and consumer affluence produce a greater concern with matters of personal status. Consequently, the argument goes, parties based on the underclass must tailor their programmes and philosophies to reflect the changing political and social attitudes of their supporters. In other words, the de-radicalization of Social Democratic parties and governments is to be understood as a *response* to pressures from 'below'. Thus, the need to revise socialist doctrines to take account of these facts was a recurrent theme of debate among Social Democratic parties in the 1950s. These 'revisionist' debates were sometimes inspired by poor electoral performances in the postwar years. Defeat was often attributed to the outdated appeal of 'cloth cap' socialism and its traditional class doctrines. The opportunities and material advantages opened up by the affluent society had weakened men's attachments to their class and to traditional political labels. As one British study expressed it:

Labour is thought of predominantly as a class party, and ... the class which it represents is – objectively and subjectively – on the wane. This stamps it with an aura of sectionalism and narrowness, at a time when people see opportunities for the advancement opening before them as never before . . . Forgotten for most people are the wretched living standards, depressions, unemployment, class rigidity, and the rest of the evils which afflicted an earlier generation . . . Labour may stand 'for the working class' but not for the increasing number who feel, rightly or wrongly, they have outgrown that label.[28]

But although the appeal to de-radicalize or 'modernize' socialist parties drew upon a number of assumptions regarding the social and political outlook of affluent workers, the validity of these assumptions has been shown to be highly questionable. If increased material prosperity led to increased political Conservatism, we should expect the most affluent workers to be the most prone to abandon their support for socialist parties. But this is not what we find. Studies of voting behaviour have established fairly conclusively that working-class support for parties of the Left does not decline as income rises; many of the most affluent workers – for example, those employed in automobile plants – show higher than average support for the Left.[29] Indeed, the striking fact of European working-class politics is the long-term stability in electoral support for Left-wing parties. As Lipset has pointed out, once a radical political party has become established as the major representative of the subordinate class loyalty to it is hardly ever eroded. 'A look at the political history of Europe indicates that no mass lower class-based political party . . . has ever disappeared or significantly declined through losing the bulk of its votes to a party on its right.'[30]

The fact that underclass support for their mass party does not greatly fluctuate over time, whatever the general level of prosperity, is bound to make us sceptical of the 'stimulus and response' theory of de-radicalization. Workers' loyalty to their party ensures that the political leadership is permitted a considerable degree of leeway in doctrinal matters. Only if support for socialist parties were more sensitive to ideological fluctuations could we accept the view that the revised version of socialism was prompted by the fear of losing the loyalty of the 'new' working class. As suggested in the previous chapter, it is much more commonly the case that members of the underclass take their political cues from their party leaders than the reverse. Thus, whether or not the underclass party proclaims a radical class doctrine on inequality is likely to be influenced more by the social situation of the *leaders* than of their traditional followers.

This was the starting point for Michels's classic analysis of socialist revisionism. Michels saw the process of de-radicalization largely as an outcome of the growth and bureaucratization of the party machine. As the socialist movement became increasingly successful in attracting supporters and members, so it fell more and more under the influence of full-time officials – men who were committed more to the performance of bureaucratic routines than to the radical transformation of society.[31] European socialist parties often became wealthy as they extended their activities into printing and publishing and the provision of various services for their members. Some, like the German S.P.D., became major employers. Those who controlled and prospered by the party machine tended to take on a somewhat more cautious view of social and political change. They, at least, had more to lose than their chains. Michels was particularly impressed by the de-radicalizing effects of the party apparatus on former working-class militants. He pointed out that proletarians who became full-time officials quickly adopted middle-class life styles and took on a different perception of society from that of the radical worker. This process of *embourgeoisement* affected not only working-class party officials but also working-class political leaders. Socialist M.P.s of proletarian origin were, in Michels's view, especially prone to disavow their radical heritage upon being drawn into the higher social circles of parliamentary life. He suggested that socialist leaders of middle-class origin were much more likely to retain their radical commitments – partly because, unlike their proletarian counterparts, they were not experiencing rapid upward mobility. Also middle-class radical leaders had cut themselves off decisively from their class or origin and were therefore more ideologically committed to their class of political adoption.

It is difficult to be sure how far the de-radicalization of underclass parties can be attributed to the *embourgeoisement* of their leaders. If Michels were right in his speculation about the radical propensities of proletarian and *bourgeois* leaders, we could assume that socialist parties would become more militant as the proportion of middle-class leaders increased. Yet we do not really find this to be so. The leadership of European Social Democratic parties has become increasingly *bourgeois* in modern times. Thus, in Britain, only 30 per cent of Labour M.P.s in the 1966 Parliament had manual working-class backgrounds. As the Table below indicates, there has been a long-term trend in this direction ever since the party established itself as a powerful electoral force and potential government.

TABLE 4.6 *Social background of Labour M.P.s*
Percentage of Labour M.P.s of working-class origin since 1918.

	%
1918–1935	72
1945	41
1951	45
1959	35
1964	30

Source : Glennerster.[32]

Similarly, according to a recent study of the German socialist movement since 1945:

The SPD is . . . ruled by a coalition of thoroughly expert, but thoroughly middle class, functionaries, managers, professional Länder politicians and dominated by its federal parliamentary wing. Thus the 'bourgeoisification' of the leadership, so often commented on by political sociologists in the past, has been completed. Although manual workers make up a majority of ordinary members they find no representation at the top of the party.[33]

But these changes in the social composition of underclass political leadership cannot be said to have halted or even checked the tendencies towards de-radicalization. On the contrary, some of the most fundamental revisions of socialist doctrine have taken place under predominantly middle-class leadership. In all fairness to Michels, however, it must be said that his statement would seem to be quite valid for the early period of the socialist movement, when it was regarded as a serious threat to *bourgeois* institutions. Under these conditions, middle-class recruits to socialism would be likely to be of a rather different type from those attracted to the party only *after* its waning radicalism had made it more acceptable to the dominant class.

As Michels himself characteristically expressed it, 'when we change the soil we change the quality of the fruit'.[34] There thus appears to be a series of separate stages to the de-radicalization process. It is probably set in train by the *embourgeoisement* of proletarian leaders and by the bureaucratization of the party apparatus in the manner described by Michels. This phase often seems to coincide with the party's transition from a revolutionary movement to a movement of radical reform through Parliament. Once the party has accepted the rules of the parliamentary game the way is then open for the second phase of de-radicalization – that brought about by the influx of 'moderate' middle-class leaders and cadres. The process thus becomes a cumulative one. The greater the inflow, of *bourgeois* recruits, the less militant the party becomes, so making it even more attractive to those who favour the interpretation of equality along meritocratic and wel-fare lines. And so on . . .

The middle-class impact on socialist ideology may be felt not only through the exercise of underclass leadership, but also through its strategic electoral position. This is particularly the case where the size or the distribution or the religious affiliations of the working class make it unlikely that the socialist party could win power by relying on the support of this section of society alone. Various factors associated with the social make-up of the underclass have combined, in many countries, to prevent the socialists from gaining more that a large minority of votes – the problem of the 'one-third barrier'. Faced with this dilemma, socialist parties have often attempted to win the support of lower white-collar groups – salaried employees in particular. Even among Social Democratic parties with Marxist antece-dents this raised few ideological objections because the property-less salariat was held to be in the same class position as the manual worker. The fact, too, that the trend in industrial socie-ties is for the manual working class to get smaller in size while the proportion of white-collar employees increases, gave an additional impetus to the socialists' attempts to broaden the social bases of their support. This attempt to win middle-class electoral support may have been one further factor contributing to the de-radicalization of socialist parties. One reason for this is that white-collar workers tend not to define their social and economic interests as identical to those of manual workers. This is partly because, as we have already seen, they do in fact enjoy a somewhat more advantageous position in the reward structure. Consequently, their support for a socialist party is likely to stem from a different conception of equality from that of industrial workers. It seems likely that salaried employees would be more attracted to an ideology proclaiming equality of opportunity, and reward on the basis of merit, than one advocating the levelling of rewards and the moral equality of manual and non-manual contributions to the social good.

In a way, the need to court white-collar approval and support might be said to have provided Social Democratic leaders with the political rationale for revising socialist doctrines along lines to which they themselves were already predisposed. At any rate, the history of European socialism certainly does not suggest that party leaders were forced reluctantly to jettison radical programmes for the sake of the middle-class vote. Indeed, in countries such as Britain and Sweden, where the size and disposition of the working class has made reliance on the middle-class vote somewhat less of an issue, the same type of political transformation has occurred as elsewhere. This strongly suggests that the main thrust of de-radicalization has come about less as a result of changes in the class composition of the electorate than as a result of the 'political acculturation' of underclass party leaders. Michels's discussion of the changing outlook of party leaders was expressed mainly in terms of their *embourgeoisement*. But developments in Social Democratic parties since Michels's time suggest that political acculturation is not simply a product of upward social mobility. Technically, it would be quite possible for underclass leaders of lowly origin to adopt middle-class life styles without necessarily adopting *bourgeois* political values. What perhaps matters much more than this type of socialization is the normative pressure imposed on those who assume positions of authority in the state. No socialist party had won power at the time Michels was writing. In modern Europe, in contrast, almost every socialist party has been involved in government, whether as the sole governing party or, more commonly, as a junior coalition partner. Underclass leaders have thus become intimately involved in the management of a social order which their party had once pledged to dismantle. This experience would seem to have eroded still further any remaining commitment to radical egalitarianism. This has little to do with the political effects of *embourgeoisement*, since most Social Democratic leaders are now middle-class before they assume office. Rather, it is to do with the fact that the administration of the state brings them into direct and continuous contact with the representatives of dominant class institutions, whose necessary co-operation is likely to be made contingent upon the exercise of power in an orthodox or 'responsible' way. The pluralist structure of modern capitalist society ensures that there are many sources of institutional power outside Parliament; since most of these are based on the dominant class they impose effective restraints on governments which seek to change the rules governing the allocation of rewards. Socialists' commitment to parliamentary methods really entails acceptance of the limited powers of socialist governments to change the system of inequalities. Governments based on the underclass party are thus in a sense constrained to adopt moderate rather than radical programmes by their very awareness of the limitations placed on their actual political power. In this situation, socialist governments or parties can still advocate reforms, but they will tend to define as 'realistic' only those reforms which can be carried through within the framework of a modern capitalist order. Examples of this strategy already referred to are those designed to improve the opportunity structure and social welfare of low status groups. Similarly, increased material benefits for such groups are held to depend more on increased productivity than on class redistribution. As Professor Galbraith has pointed out, the pressure to achieve increasing rates of aggregate output can be seen as an alternative to pressure for redistribution. By increasing the size of the national cake, a bigger slice can be allocated to the underclass without enlarging its *proportion* of the whole.[35] All governments are thus greatly concerned to maintain or increase productivity, but perhaps socialist governments more than most. This is because they have a special obligation to improve the economic lot of the underclass. And to make this contingent upon an increase in national wealth (for example by tying wages to productivity) is to declare that existing class differentials are accepted as legitimate.

It would in fact be true to say that the entire field of wages and industrial relations is one fraught with particular tensions for socialist governments. This is because, on the one hand, they are committed to the rules governing distribution, while on the other, they are ideologically committed to improving the material level of those who stand to lose by the application of the rules. Dilemmas of this kind also face trade union leaders who have been absorbed into the apparatus of the state. V. L. Allen has pointed out that, in Britain, union leaders were represented on only twelve government committees in 1939; by 1948 they were on sixty, and by the early 1950s they were on more than eighty.[36] Allen suggests that, as a result, union leaders have come under heavy pressure to act in a 'responsible' and 'statesmanlike' manner. This is understood to mean that they will act to safeguard the 'national interest', and not the class interests of their members. In Holland, trade union leaders are even more closely involved than their British counterparts in the management of government incomes policies. According to Professor Goudsblom:

In return for this exclusive recognition, they are expected to act 'constructively' and 'responsibly' . . . In the immediate postwar period of recovery they have helped to maintain a low wage level so as to further industrial investment . . . In the years of prosperity following economic recovery they have perpetuated the same policy of loyalty and restraint . . . Moreover in some prosperous industries hard pressed by a labour shortage, wage raises that seem easily obtainable are not materializing because the unions reject them as incompatible with the public interest.[37]

This tendency for underclass leaders, in socialist parties or trade unions, to redefine their duty as the protection of the national interest obviously undermines their position as class representatives. To withdraw pressure for redistribution in favour of some other abstract principle is to confer an advantage on the dominant class. Clearly, in a class-stratified society the very notion of a 'national' interest is highly problematic. In terms of income distribution, what does not go to the subordinate class goes to the dominant class instead.

The adoption of this type of outlook is particularly likely when underclass leaders are incorporated in the management of the state. This is a common occurrence at the present time, so that the political process analysed by Michels has continued at an accelerated rate. What is so important about the Michelian analysis of de-radicalization is its illustration of the fact that changing attitudes to inequality on the part of underclass leaders are not necessarily determined by the facts of inequality. The balance of class advantages in West European societies cannot be said to have undergone a major change in the last three decades or so. In this same period, however, most European socialist parties have taken major steps towards the abandonment of radical doctrines. The clear implication of this is that the parties' changing approaches to inequality are attributable at least as much to the social influences at work on the underclass leadership as to changes in the structure of class advantages.

To some extent, the developments in Social Democratic parties outlined above have also occurred in Communist parties, particularly where the latter have replaced the former as the mass party of the working class. Thus, European Communist parties have, in the main, abandoned early revolutionary aims in favour of a constitutional approach to social change. But it would not be true to say that they have discarded their commitment to dismantle the reward and property structure of modern capitalism. In this respect, at least, they envisage a far more radical redistribution of advantages than that advocated by Social Democrats. It is this fact which, in part, ensures that the underclass in societies like France and Italy are somewhat less amenable to their subordinate position than are the underclass in societies where Social Democrats are the mass party.

Whether or not the Communist parties will eventually become as de-radicalized as the Social Democratic parties is of course open to speculation. But what is of immediate interest here is the possible effect on the stratification order of Communist party rule. In Eastern Europe, Communist-controlled governments have been in office for the past twenty-five years, and in the Soviet Union more than twice as long. It is therefore of some interest to examine the structure of inequalities in these societies, and to consider how far they differ from those of their Western capitalist neighbours.

5 The Problem of Classes in Socialist Society

In turning our attention to inequalities in societies of the Soviet or socialist type we are confronted by an initial problem of definition. To what extent, it may be asked, can socialist society be regarded as having a class system, in the sense in which the term is used to describe the reward structure typical of modern capitalism? There is a good deal of literature, scholarly and polemical, devoted to this issue, and it may be useful to begin with a brief examination of the major propositions put forward in support of contending views. It should be emphasized at the outset that the debate over the problem of class in socialist society is by no means an empty wrangle over terminology; it does in fact raise a number of substantive issues which are of direct relevance to our understanding of the stratification process in industrial society.

One of the key propositions to emerge in this debate is that which declares socialist society to be classless. Support for this thesis comes from two opposed intellectual and political sources – one associated with Marxist orthodoxy and the other with pluralist or democratic theory. The orthodox Marxist view holds quite simply that class divisions are rooted in private property relationships; and since in socialist society the private ownership of productive property does not exist, there can be no classes. This view does not deny that material and social differences exist between different groups, such as industrial workers and intellectuals; but it is argued that such groups are not in a mutually antagonistic relationship with one another since they share a similar status with respect to the resources of production. In a society which does not confer a special legal status upon property owners, there can be no inherent antagonisms of a class kind equivalent to those which emerge between a proletariat and a *bourgeoisie*. The social and material differentiation which arises under socialism tends to bring about the formation not of social classes but of what are often termed 'non-antagonistic strata'. Moreover, differences between these strata are seen as continually narrowing as society progresses further along the road to full Communism. Thus, although there may appear to be certain surface similarities between the reward structure of modern capitalist and socialist societies, what sharply distinguishes them is the fact that the latter is in a *transitional stage* towards a new type of social order, whereas the former is not.[1]

East European sociologists often elaborate upon this thesis by suggesting that the high degree of social fluidity in their societies militates against the formation of clear class boundaries. Inequalities exist, and will continue to exist into the foreseeable future; but these are seen to be related to positional differentiation, and are not regarded as indices of class formation. Present rewards and privileges form a graduated continuum, and there are not the same clear-cut breaks between one point in the scale and another, such as we find under conditions of capitalism. In other words, the 'vertical' distribution of rewards does not produce a 'horizontal' clustering of positions which is the characteristic feature of class structure.

Support for the classlessness thesis also comes from a number of Western scholars who approach the problem from a rather different perspective. For these writers, like Raymond Aron, William Kornhauser and Robert Feldmesser, the most distinctive feature of Soviet-type societies is the cleavage between the Party and the people. So fundamental, it is argued, is the social gulf between Party personnel and the mass of non-Party citizens that it tends to eradicate all other potential divisions. The coercive activities of the Party apparatus and the secret police permeate all spheres of daily life to such a degree that fear of the Party becomes the central fact of existence for most men and their families. Under these conditions, when people are continually threatened with the possibility of arrest, sentiments of a class character do not readily emerge.[2] Differences in social background, income, occupation and the like, have a greatly reduced influence on behaviour and outlook in the face of more pressing anxieties and concerns. In some respects, the situation might be said to be analogous to that in societies with sharp racial cleavages. In South Africa or the Deep South the distinction between black and white is so all-encompassing as to hinder the formation of well defined boundaries and sentiments of a purely class character. In socialist society, however, classes are not merely inhibited from becoming fully formed because of the salience of other social factors; rather the Party seeks actively to *prevent* their formation because classes, like any other independent social collectivity or organization, might attempt to challenge the Party's authority. In particular, the Party would wish to prevent the crystallization of a 'managerial class' of the kind predicted by James Burnham, since this could become a powerful social force in its own right and so free itself from the dictates of the Party apparatus. Thus, all this is seen as resulting in a society which is not class-stratified, but is instead split between an *élite* of Party personnel on the one hand, and a relatively undifferentiated mass of non-Party personnel on the other. In this type of social structure there are no major social groups or institutions intermediate between the citizen and the state; the masses are socially isolated, alienated, and demoralized, the objects of manipulation by an all-powerful state and Party apparatus.[3]

Further evidence of classlessness, as seen in this same perspective, is detected in the lack of normative and cultural differentiation. Whereas in Western society members of different social classes typically exhibit marked variations in outlook and values, homogeneity of outlook is the keynote of socialist society. As Feldmesser puts it, the 'hierarchical strata of Soviet society should be more nearly and more often alike in their attitudes than their counterparts in other industrial societies'. And he goes on to suggest that there is 'a remarkably low relationship between hierarchical position and many of the elements of ideology which we customarily associate with class-differentiated structures'.[4]

What is seen as the key contrast between socialist and Western systems of stratification is, ultimately, the structure of political power. Western societies are seen to be characterized by a pluralistic distribution of power in which the various institutional spheres are guaranteed legal autonomy. Socialist societies, on the other hand, have a totalitarian authority structure in which the Party monopolizes all decision-making processes and denies independence to any major institution. Under the former arrangement classes can develop quite freely, while under the latter they cannot. As Goldthorpe puts it, in his paraphrase of Aron, 'class stratification and a monistic political system are to be regarded as incompatibles'.[5]

The classlessness thesis, from whichever angle it has been advanced, has not met with universal support. It has, for example, been rejected by many who would describe themselves as Marxists whose objections rest upon what they see to be the essentially similar, exploitative nature of both capitalist and Soviet-type societies. In both social systems a small privileged class expropriates the fruits of other men's labours, either through the legal ownership of productive resources or through political control over such resources.[6] The orthodox Marxist's distinction between ownership and control of productive property is denied by certain 'revisionist' Marxists. Djilas, for example, has suggested that a 'new class' of exploiters has arisen in socialist society as a result of their formal, if not legal, ownership of state resources.[7] For Djilas, those who effectively control property and who have rights over the disposition of goods and services, are in a real sense the 'owners' of property. In this respect there could be said to be little significant difference between a propertied *bourgeoisie* of the capitalist variety and a 'new class' of Communist Party bureaucrats such as we find at the apex of socialist society. The latter can be considered as much a class as the former in so far as it stands in an antagonistic and exploitative relationship to those who must sell their labour power. So long as the industrial workforce lacks control over political and industrial institutions, what we have is not socialism but simply 'state capitalism', with all that this implies in the way of inequality between the classes.

A somewhat more oblique rejection of the classlessness thesis is contained in the writings of those who see industrial societies of East and West as converging towards a similar type or pattern. Scholars like Galbraith, Kerr, and Inkeles, among others, have suggested that the forces of modern industrialism impose certain uniformities on society whatever its political ideology and institutions.[8] Technological advances and the demands of economic progress give rise to a similar reward structure in both types of society; the organization of industry, the system of education and the occupational structure, are all highly responsive to the pressures of modernization. Under these conditions the class system tends to lose many of the harsh features associated with the earlier phase of industrialism; but classes as such are not necessarily scheduled for disappearance under either capitalism or socialism.

These then are the various propositions which have, in one form or another, been advanced in connection with the problem of class in socialist society. Some of them are couched in more subtle terms than in the presentation above, and some have a much sharper polemical edge; all of them rely for their persuasive force on the acceptance of certain unstated moral assumptions. What we need to do here, as in the previous chapter, is to review the issues raised in the light of such evidence as is available. This is not to say that the problem can be settled in any final way; it cannot, partly because certain of the issues raised are not open to empirical solution and partly because the evidence for those which are is not at present available. However, we are by no means completely in the dark, and it is indeed now possible to discern a certain pattern in the bits and pieces of evidence which are at our disposal. No doubt this pattern will change shape as new social facts come to light; but this of course is a hazard which is not confined to the study of socialist society.

2

In considering the reward structure of European socialist societies it is useful to draw a distinction between the period immediately following the Communist Party's succession to office and the more recent period of consolidation and industrial advance. The former period, commonly referred to as that of 'socialist reconstruction', heralded a series of fundamental social reforms, often of a markedly egalitarian nature. Egalitarianism was especially evident in the introduction of various fiscal reforms, most obviously those affecting income distribution. In the Soviet Union, for example, following the seizure of power by the Bolsheviks, wage differentials between blue- and white-collar workers were drastically reduced, and in some cases disappeared completely. In Poland, Yugoslavia, Hungary and Czechoslovakia, among other East European states, similar incomes policies were pursued by the newly-established regimes. In addition, manual workers in these countries were often favoured in the allocation of housing and food rations, while members of the former *bourgeoisie* experienced various social punishments and deprivations. Those who had held positions of authority under the *ancien régime* were frequently demoted to more routine tasks and replaced by those who were more politically reliable. The latter were generally drawn from the ranks of those who had served in the pre-war clandestine Communist parties, or who had fought in the underground resistance against German occupation. Generally they were men of fairly humble social origin, ex-peasants and industrial workers with a sprinkling of radical intellectuals. Thus, for a small minority the seizure of power entailed rapid upward social mobility via the Party into top administrative, political, managerial, and similar positions of authority.

At the same time social changes of a more broadly based kind were also being initiated. One major example was the crash educational programme designed to create a new intelligentsia from the young members of formerly underprivileged groups of workers and peasants. This called for sweeping reforms in the educational system, particularly the universities and similar institutes of higher learning. In pre-war Eastern Europe, as in most of Western Europe today, the universities were largely the preserve of the middle and upper classes. In the period of social-ist reconstruction this situation was dramatically changed by the introduction of selective systems designed to favour students from proletarian families. This was generally done by fixing a quota on the proportion of candidates from white-collar families, and by accepting large numbers of workers' and peasants' children who lacked formal entrance qualifications. In this manner, the class composition of universities and similar institutes underwent a radical transformation. In some states, students from manual backgrounds soon outnumbered those from non-manual homes, but even where this did not occur heavy inroads were still made into the traditional educational privileges of the latter.[9] Taken all in all, the overhaul of the educational system, the introduction of an egalitarian incomes-structure, and the expropriation of landed estates and industrial property, served to alter substantially the former balance of class advantages. This phase in the political economy of socialist societies offers clear testimony to the role of ideology in bringing about fundamental changes in the entire stratification order. The contrast with the impact of Labour and Social Democratic governments on capitalist society is a vivid one.

Certain of the egalitarian tendencies of the reconstruction phase appear to have been halted, or even reversed, in later periods. This is not to say that inequalities on the Western scale began to be discernible, but rather that the impetus towards social and material levelling appears to have become noticeably weaker. This has been more so in some societies than in others; in the Soviet Union, for example, the reaction against early egalitarian measures was much sharper than it has been else-where in Eastern Europe. In the early 1930s Stalin launched an attack upon the equalization principles which had formed the basis of Soviet incomes policies for the first decade or so of Bolshevik rule. Stalin declared that greater material incentives and privileges had to be offered to those who were engaged on skilled work, including the newly emerging managerial and technical cadres. Without sharp income differentials, he argued, there would be no stimulus to learn the skills and assume the responsibilities required in a rapidly industrializing society. A fierce campaign was waged against *uravnilovka* ('equality-mongering'), and an end was called for to the stigmatization of administrative and other white-collar employees. As a result of Stalin's measures the income structure of the Soviet Union became one of the most differentiated and complex of any industrial country. The trend towards increasing inequality continued throughout the 1940s; the inheritance tax of 1926, which had imposed steeply progressive death duties on estates, was repealed. Reforms in income tax laws were also highly favourable to the best paid groups in Soviet society.[10] All this ensured that the most privileged groups could not only accumulate wealth in their own lifetime, but could also pass it on to their heirs.

Following Stalin's death, however, and his denunciation at the 20th Party Congress, many of the trends towards increasing inequality were put into reverse. Minimum wages were raised and increases were granted to workers in medium-income brackets; differentials between various skill categories were also narrowed. Income tax reforms eased the burden on lower income groups by becoming more steeply progressive.[11] In the other European socialist states fluctuations between egalitarianism and steep inequality do not appear to have been as extreme as they were in the Soviet Union, although exact comparisons are not possible because of the different time-spans involved. It is quite clear, however, that a similar reaction against income levelling did set in among most of these other states, with similar political campaigns against 'equality-mongering'. Again, however, it would seem that the increasing inequality of the 1950s was halted by government action; by the early 1960s blue-collar workers had been restored to a more favourable position. As the United Nations survey of European incomes has shown, some narrowing of differentials between higher white-collar groups and blue-collar workers was indicated in 1964, while the latter had actually overtaken the lower white-collar employees in all countries except Poland.

TABLE 5.1 *Income differentials of occupational categories in industry, Eastern Europe 1964*

(Workers' earnings .. 100·0.)

	Bulgaria	Hungary	Czecho-slovakia	Poland	U.S.S.R.
Manual workers	100·0	100·0	100·0	100·0	100·0
Clerical and admin. staff	98·5	94·6	84·3	105·4	84·0
Engineering and technical staff	142·8	153·3	130·3	164·9	144·0

Source: U.N., *Economic Survey of Europe in 1965*, Part II, Table 8.18.

To some extent the narrowing of income differentials has come about as a result of changes in the occupational structure. As more qualified men become available because of improved educational opportunities, the scarcity value attaching to skill is reduced; indeed the problem is sometimes one of recruiting men to perform menial labouring tasks. Under these conditions there are sound economic grounds for lowering the rewards for skilled work and increasing those for unskilled. In this respect the narrowing of differentials in the Soviet Union and other heavily industrialized socialist states can be partly explained in terms of the same economic forces which produced a similar trend in Western Europe. However, although factors of supply and demand obviously make themselves felt upon the socialist income structure, and upon the economy in general, it would be misleading to claim that the market is the governing mechanism of reward allocation. It is certainly the case that in Eastern, as in Western, Europe the occupational reward hierarchy tends to correspond to the hierarchy of skill and expertise. However, it must also be noted that non-market criteria play a significant part in wage determination in the command economies. Thus in the wage tariffs drawn up by central planning agencies, factors such as the physical strenuousness of work, health hazards, and similar non-market considerations are taken into account in arriving at a final figure. Table 5.2 shows differences in average wage rates in Hungary according to the 'heaviness' of work, with skill level held constant.

TABLE 5.2 *Differences in basic wages according to skill and work conditions, Hungary 1964*

	Unskilled	Semi-skilled
(Industrial average)	(100·0)	(100·0)
Light manual	91·5	92·4
Normal manual	98·4	98·1
Heavy manual	110·6	104·9

Source: U.N., *Economic Survey of Europe in 1965*, Part II, Table 8.5.

In addition, wage tariffs are also affected by the planning priorities accorded to the different economic sectors. Thus wages in high priority sectors such as building and construction are generally well above those in less 'productive' branches such as trade and communal services.[12] The fact that attributes of this kind are taken into account in the allocation of rewards indicates the continuing importance of political or ideological constraints upon the market. This points up the fact that in a command economy the rewards system is much more responsive to manipulation by the central authority than it is in a market-based economy. This of course holds not only for income distribution but for a whole range of other material, social and symbolic benefits. Given this important distinction between the two systems it may at this point be useful to ask to what extent broad similarities in the organization of production, and in the occupational order, can be said to have produced a basically similar class system. In particular, could it be maintained that the manual/non-manual cleavage, which characterizes the class structure of capitalist society, also pertains to socialist society? At first blush there does appear to be a good case for advancing such a claim, particularly if we have in mind the obvious contrasts between such groups as industrial workers and factory directors. But parallels of this type, however instructive in other ways, would not be sufficient to clinch the argument for a socialist class system similar to the Western model. To begin with, there appear to be certain relevant differences in the rank ordering of broad occupational categories. In many socialist societies highly skilled or craft manual workers enjoy a higher position in the scale of material and status rewards than do lower white-collar employees. The relatively depressed status of the latter, compared with their Western counterparts, is indicated by the scale of income differentials set out in Table 5.1. These figures do not bring out the differences between skilled and unskilled blue-collar workers, but it is largely due to the higher incomes of the former that manual workers as a whole are seen to enjoy a better material position than lower white-collar employees. When workers' earnings are classified according to skill, then office employees and similar white-collar grades are shown to occupy an intermediate place between the skilled and unskilled manual workers. Thus, in Yugoslavia skilled workers in 1961 earned on average 25 per cent more than office staff, whereas the latter's incomes were about 35 per cent higher than those of unskilled labourers.[13] The significance of this distinction is further suggested by studies of occupational prestige in socialist countries. Sarapata and Wesolowski have shown that in Poland skilled manual positions enjoy higher social standing than do lower white-collar positions – a reverse of the situation prevailing in the pre-socialist period.[14] In Yugoslavia, too, skilled manual work is looked upon with more favour than is routine white-collar work, as measured by studies of occupational prestige and of parents' aspirations for their children.[15] In all these various studies occupations requiring higher education and professional qualifications are accorded to highest social standing, while unskilled labouring positions are invariably placed lowest in rank-order. Thus in terms of broad occupational categories the overall reward hierarchy appears to run from high to low as follows: (1) White-collar intelligentsia (i.e. professional, managerial and administrative positions). (2) Skilled manual positions. (3) Lower or unqualified white-collar positions. (4) Unskilled manual positions.

What this means is that we cannot represent the reward structure of socialist society as a dichotomous class model on exactly the Western pattern, since there is much less of an obvious 'break' between manual and non-manual positions. The lower non-manual categories in socialist society could not be said to enjoy the same kinds of status, material, and social advantages over skilled or relatively well-paid manual workers as do their counterparts in capitalist society. Consequently, they cannot really be regarded as forming the tail-end of a professional middle class in quite the same way. For example, office employees in socialist society are not generally accorded special privileges with regard to time-keeping, length of vacations, paid absenteeism, and the like. Nor can they expect to enjoy status advantages over shop floor workers in the way of separate canteens, entrances, lavatories, and so on, which serve to distinguish 'staff' from 'works' on the Western pattern.[16] In certain respects, in fact, office personnel appear to be at a disadvantage compared with men on the shop floor. This is not simply a matter of income differentials; in addition, it concerns career prospects and opportunities for promotion. In Britain, as in other Western societies, clerical employment is often regarded as the bottom rung of a ladder which leads to junior managerial positions. As such it has commonly been regarded as an avenue of mobility for men of working-class origin.[17] Manual employment does not generally offer a similar career structure, and the great majority of those who start work on the shop floor do not transform their occupational status through time.

In the Soviet Union and East Europe this situation does not prevail to quite the same extent. In the first place there seems to be no well-worn route from the general office to the managerial desk. This is largely because of the great importance attached to formal educational and technical qualifications in the appointment of managerial and other leading personnel. Those recruited to the ranks of the technical and professional intelligentsia generally arrive direct from university. This also happens to some extent in Western Europe, of course; but in Eastern Europe, and especially the Soviet Union, the proportion of graduates among new entrants to the labour force is considerably higher than it is in the rest of Europe.[18] Consequently, the chances of unqualified white-collar employees moving up into the managerial grade are that much slimmer. Where internal promotion of this kind does tend to occur is in the state administration and Party apparatus, where political qualifications are often given heavier weighting than are purely technical ones. Outside these restricted spheres, however, the demand for expertise and paper certificates makes itself felt more strongly, to the obvious disadvantage of unqualified white-collar staff.

As far as blue-collar workers are concerned, the opportunities to achieve managerial or similar status are probably no better. But where this sector of the workforce is advantaged, at least in comparison with its Western counterpart, is in the range of opportunities available for upward mobility *within* the manual class by the acquisition of new skills. The facilities for re-training workers and for improving the level of skill by on-job and vocational training are well developed in the command economies.[19] In market economies, by contrast, employers tend to be reluctant to invest heavy resources in training men since they risk losing the return on their investment through labour turnover. Calculations of this kind are clearly less relevant for the socialist firm. Thus unskilled and semi-skilled workers are provided with good opportunities for improving their material and social status without having to exchange a blue collar for a white one. Milić's study of career mobility in Yugoslavia showed that more than 80 per cent of skilled and highly skilled workers had received their training since entering employment, either through in-factory training or part-time attendance at trade schools and 'workers' universities'.[20] Similar provisions are made in the Soviet Union and elsewhere in East Europe, with beneficial effects on the life-chances of manual workers. All this indicates that the relationship between blue-collar and lower white-collar positions is not the same in socialist society as it is under capitalism. This reversal in their relative statuses means that in socialist society we cannot draw a class dividing line at the point which separates the non-manual from the manual occupational groups.

3

A further related feature of the socialist reward system is the privileged status of the white-collar intelligentsia. As Table 5.1. indicated, the income differentials between these higher white-collar grades and manual workers are everywhere wider than the differentials between workers and lower white-collar grades. In other words the most obvious break in the reward hierarchy occurs along the line separating the qualified professional, managerial and technical positions from the rest of the occupational order. Income differences are of course only one, albeit important, index of the advantaged status of the white-collar intelligentsia. In addition to their basic salary rates many of them, expecially those employed in industry, receive various bonuses and special supplements which serve to widen the gap between their economic position and that of other groups. Similarly, they tend to enjoy certain less measurable, but no less valuable, advantages such as high-quality accommodation, opportunities to travel abroad, use of official cars and state property, and other perquisites of office. The special privileges of the intelligentsia tend not to percolate down, as it were, to the routine white-collar staff as they often do in capitalist business enterprises; and this is one more reason why we cannot lump both categories of non-manual employee into the same social class. Expressed rather differently, there is a markedly greater social discontinuity between higher and lower white-collar groups under socialism than under capitalism; thus, under the former system they cannot be regarded as different segments of a broadly based 'middle class'.

The social boundary between the white-collar intelligentsia and the rest of the occupational hierarchy becomes even more clearly delineated when we take political factors into account. What is here referred to is membership of the Communist Party and the privileges which this brings. Throughout Eastern Europe, the Communist Party has been undergoing a long-term process of 'de-proletarianization'. In the reconstruction and pre-socialist periods the Party's main source of recruitment was the blue-collar workforce and the poor peasantry; but with the creation of a new white-collar *élite* the representation of these groups has declined sharply in relation to the latter's. In Yugoslavia, for example, workers and peasants accounted for almost four-fifths of the Party membership in 1948; but by 1957 they made up less than half. Figures published by the Party in 1967 show that the decline in manual representation has continued and that white-collar specialists are joining in still greater numbers. These changes in the occupational make-up of the Party have come about not simply through differential recruitment rates but also through the pattern of resignations and expulsions. In 1966 alone, more than half of all members purged were industrial workers, while 54 per cent of those who resigned voluntarily were also workers.[21] The situation in Poland is similar. In 1945 non-manual employees accounted for less than 10 per cent of the Party membership; by 1961 they made up almost 43 per cent of the total. Professor Bauman, in a later study, found that those with higher education were three times more likely to be Party members than those with only elementary schooling. Party activists were even more likely to be drawn from the ranks of white-collar experts; among technicians and engineers, 1 in 15 was an activist, as against 1 in 75 skilled workers, and only 1 in 198 unskilled workers.[22] In Czechoslovakia, about 60 per cent of Party members were manual workers in the early period of socialist rule, a figure which had already fallen to about 36 per cent by 1956. There has been a similar tendency in Hungary, where technical and professional qualifications are increasingly demanded of candidates for Party membership.[23] This process of 'de-proletarianization' has of course had longer to run in the Soviet Union, so it is not altogether surprising to learn that, according to Schwarz's calculations, one in every three white-collar specialists with higher education is now a Party member. Schwarz's conclusion that workers are being 'steadily thrust into the background within the communist party',[24] could stand as a verdict on the situation in East Europe generally.

The fact that the white-collar intelligentsia has become increasingly identified with the Communist Party tends to enhance this group's privileged position in society. Most of their advantages do of course derive from their occupational status, and in this respect they share a functionally similar position to the professional and managerial categories in Western society. At the same time, however, their fusion with the Communist Party provides them with a variety of other supplementary advantages. These are sometimes of a material kind, but more often perhaps they are more intangible and consist in such things as the ability to pull strings and win favours from local decision-makers. Thus, whether it is a matter of getting the best theatre tickets, or ensuring a place for one's child at a good school or university, Party membership and the network of informal contacts it provides can often make all the difference between success and failure. No less important is the fact that a good Party record helps to smooth a man's progress in his career and to make him a potential candidate for the most responsible posts. Thus, the greater an occupational group's involvement with the Party the greater its claims to those social and other benefits which do not directly stem from the division of labour. In this respect the white-collar intelligentsia in socialist society has access to a source of reward which has no real functional equivalent in Western society.

The fact that the intelligentsia stands out as being socially and materially advantaged *and* so closely tied in with the Party would seem to reinforce the case for singling them out as a dominant class. Some writers, as pointed out at the beginning of this chapter, have wished to confine this notion to those who occupy positions of political authority in the state apparatus.

Djilas, for example, defined the 'new class' as 'those who have special privileges and economic preference because of the *administrative* monopoly they hold'.[25] That is, it was the men who held political or Party office on a full-time basis who were the main beneficiaries of the system, rather than those in professional or managerial positions who were simply Party *members*. However, this distinction is not an easy one to sustain. Full time Party functionaries are increasingly drawn from the ranks of those with higher education; in some cases they have formerly been employed in industry or in other jobs outside the Party apparatus. Similarly, *apparatchiki* sometimes change career in mid-stream and enter managerial or non-Party administrative posts. Bauman, discussing the situation in Poland, thus argues that white-collar experts and Party functionaries cannot now be 'separated into two classes with different and conflicting interests. On the contrary, many intrinsic attributes of their respective social positions and roles testify to their basic sociological unity'.[26] This unity will probably increase as the veteran ex-partisan, ex-peasant functionaries retire and give way to younger men who have passed through the same system of higher education as the professional and managerial cadres. If, therefore, we are seeking to identify a dominant social class in this type of society it is more realistic to treat the white-collar intelligentsia and the *apparatchiki* as a single social entity. We can of course recognize differences between them, but these are probably no greater than the differences we find between the various groups which make up the dominant class of capitalist society. Djilas himself, for all his emphasis on the political component of the 'new class', recognized that it extended well beyond the boundaries of the Party apparatus. As he put it, 'The party makes the class, but the class grows as a result and uses the party as a basis. The class grows stronger, while the party grows weaker'.[27]

Djilas, in common with many 'revisionists' or neo-Marxists, was concerned to point up parallels between the 'new class' and the property-owning class in capitalist society. He argued that the class based on the Communist Party enjoyed virtually the same rights over property as a traditional *bourgeoisie*. If ownership is defined as rights over the use and products of collective property, and not simply *legal* entitlement, then the dominant class of socialist society can be conceived of as a propertied class. In this sense it has the same exploitative status as its capitalist counterpart; both enjoy a materially privileged position based upon expropriation of the surplus value created by the subordinate class. If, then, we replace the legal definition of ownership with a sociological one, the similarity between a classic *bourgeoisie* and the 'new class' of socialist society is thrown into high relief.

This argument is in many ways an appealing one, but certain qualifications must be entered against it in its present form. In the first place, given the absence of legal title to productive property there can be no inheritance within the family from one generation to the next. The privileges of the 'new class' rest heavily upon political office, and office cannot be transferred from father to son in the way that private property can. What gives an ideal-typical *bourgeoisie* its distinctive class character is its high degree of social self-recruitment through time; and this is facilitated by the legal transfer of property and wealth to family descendants. Under these conditions the propertied class tends to develop a certain cultural distinctiveness which serves to reinforce further its social exclusiveness. This does not accurately portray the situation in socialist society. At this point, then, the analogy between the two types of 'propertied' class appears to break down.

Now it can of course be countered that members of the 'new class' can transfer *other* kinds of advantages to their offspring which will ensure them a privileged social position. Most obvious among these is higher education. If the progeny of the 'new class' become educationally advantaged, as a result of their favourable home backgrounds, then they will enjoy the kind of head start over others which, under a different system, the inheritance of wealth can provide. Furthermore, if, with the economists, we consider higher education as a form of 'investment' which brings a high rate of return, the analogy between property and educational inheritance becomes even closer. Whatever kind of advantage is handed down, be it property or education, the privileged position of dominant class members is inherited by their own offspring. If we frame Djilas's argument in these terms, the case for treating the 'new class' as essentially similar to the *bourgeoisie* is somewhat stronger. Evidence from Eastern Europe does in fact suggest that those born into the white-collar intelligentsia tend to do well in the competition for academic honours. As a result they enter occupations similar to those of their parents; very few become manual workers or lower white-collar employees. Separate figures are not usually available for the sons and daughters of the *apparatchiki*, but it seems unlikely that their achievements differ very much from those of other children of the 'new class'. Where formal qualifications are a passport to privileged occupations, the educational system is almost bound to confer an advantage on well-born children – at least in the absence of state policies designed to offset the latter's natural advantages. As has already been pointed out, such policies were pursued in the reconstruction period in the form of positive discrimination towards those with proletarian credentials. In more recent times, however, this type of selection procedure has been operated with much less stringency. Consequently, children of the 'new class' are not faced with the same handicaps as the children of the former *bourgeoisie*.

4

All this does serve to highlight apparent similarities in the reward system of socialist and capitalist societies. But we should not press the similarities too far since there are also crucial variations to consider, apart from those already touched upon. Most significant among these, perhaps, is the range and extent of upward mobility in socialist society. Although it is true that the offspring of privileged groups can usually bank upon reproducing their parents' status, it is equally true that the less well born have favourable opportunities for social advancement. The increase in the number of higher white-collar positions throughout Eastern Europe has been sufficiently great to absorb not merely the progeny of the intelligentsia, but also many of those from peasants' and workers' families. In other words, the 'new class' cannot be considered a closed and socially exclusive group which has put up barriers to recruitment from 'below'. Indeed, there is some evidence that recruitment into this class from lower strata is sufficiently great, in absolute terms, to outweigh the number of self-recruits, though in percentage terms the former type movement is considerably less. A 1963 study in Hungary, for example, showed that almost 77 per cent of managerial, administrative, and professional positions were filled by men and women of worker and peasant origin.[28] Since this category also includes party functionaries of various kinds, we can assume that many of these appointments were political ones dating back to the reconstruction period. A somewhat better indication of mobility as affected by educational rather than political qualifications is provided by data on the social background of the intelligentsia proper. Even here, 53 per cent of doctors, scientists, engineers, and the like were from peasants' and manual workers' families; this is remarkably high by West European standards and serves to demonstrate the impact of earlier reforms in higher education.[29] In Yugoslavia the picture is similar. As recorded in the 1960 census, 61·8 per cent of those in managerial and administrative posts were of manual origin, again no doubt reflecting the weight attached to political criteria in filling posts of this type. The social composition of the higher professions was, as in the case of Hungary, less markedly proletarian, although still relatively high at 49 per cent.[30] '*Élite*' mobility on this scale means that the 'new class' is continually replenishing itself from among the offspring of less privileged groups. As Djilas noted, 'The new class is actually being created from the lowest and broadest strata of the people, and is in constant motion. Although it is sociologically possible to prescribe who belongs to the new class, it is difficult to do so; for the new class melts into and spills over into the people, into other lower classes, and is constantly changing.'[31]

Entry into the top layers of the dominant class is far more difficult for those born in the subordinate class in a capitalist society. This must be seen as a further point of contrast between the two systems, and one which has far-reaching implications for the stratification order in general. This is particularly the case with regard to the normative aspects of class inequality. In societies where the dominant class shows a high degree of self-recruitment and social exclusiveness, normative patterns of a 'defensive' kind tend to emerge among the subordinate class, or at least large sectors of it. Where the latter perceive the opportunity structure to be weighted against them, they will tend to generate a normative system in which the values associated with success and achievement are strongly de-emphasized. As suggested in Chapter 3, subordinate value systems generally promote various modes of accommodation to disprivileged status, and thus give little support to norms of occupational and educational advancement. Orientations of this kind arise from collective experiences of the opportunity structure and from the social knowledge that few of those born into low status groups can expect to move up into privileged positions. Once this type of value system becomes crystallized it tends to have a confirmatory feed-back effect on the factual order; that is, it leads to the negation of such opportunities as do exist by stripping away motivational supports which are necessary to transform opportunities into achievements.

In socialist societies, negative or defensive value-orientations of this character do not appear to have taken root among the relatively disprivileged. One indication of this is the fact that parents' ambitions for their children are pitched much higher in socialist than in capitalist society. A striking feature of the former is the extent to which commitment to higher education and the desire for professional careers have spread among members of lower strata.[32] Among the young particularly the desire is to move not simply into non-manual positions, but into the ranks of the intelligentsia. Lower white-collar or office employment is not generally regarded as a desirable goal for ambitious working-class youth as it has traditionally been in the West; indeed it is doubtful, on the grounds already stated, whether it could be regarded as an upward move at all, except perhaps for children of the poor peasantry. The fact that achievement orientations appear to have percolated down to lower-status youth can be taken as a useful index of the openness of the stratification order. It is at any rate highly unlikely that this normative outlook could have developed if it were not factually the case that the opportunity structure was a favourable one. As Blau and Duncan have argued, optimistic attitudes concerning mobility chances cannot be sustained in the face of continuously disconfirming evidence.[33] This is not to say of course that the 'level' of optimism is always exactly in accordance with the 'level' of opportunity. Indeed it does appear to be the case in socialist society that the number of young people wishing to enter higher white-collar positions is considerably greater than the number of posts likely to be available. The gross numbers of those moving up into the intelligentsia from manual and peasant families will still be large by Western standards, although they will represent only a fairly small minority of the whole. This of course is especially so in those societies which have a very large manual and peasant population and a small intelligentsia; under these conditions, even modest percentage shifts from the former to the latter represent large additions to the intelligentsia measured in numerical terms. What, perhaps, give mobility rates in socialist society their special significance is the fact that they indicate large-scale movements across the entire range of the reward hierarchy, not merely the interchange of personnel at the class margins. Because upward mobility is frequently of an '*élite*', and not simply a 'mass', kind it is likely to have an important influence on the popular perception of the opportunity structure. Social promotion to professional and managerial positions is likely to have greater 'visibility' than more modest forms of mobility. If the occupants of leading positions in industrial, administrative, political, and other spheres are known to have risen from humble beginnings (and there is certainly no reluctance to display a proletarian pedigree) then they stand as confirming evidence for the openness of the stratification order. And the spread of social knowledge that low birth is no barrier to advancement is likely to have self-fulfilling consequences.

What this amounts to saying is that European socialist societies appear to display less normative differentiation along class lines than do Western societies. Undoubtedly some such differentiation does occur among the former, although it seems doubtful whether we could accurately refer to a distinctive 'working-class subculture' analogous to that we find among the subordinate class under capitalism. Similarly, there is little evidence for the emergence among the 'new class' of a distinctive culture, accent, mode of dress, and the like, comparable to that produced by the English upper class or French *haute bourgeoisie*. Cultural and normative differentiation of this order probably cannot really develop if members of lower strata are continuously recruited in large numbers into the dominant class; a mass influx of the low born is almost bound to dilute anything resembling an elitist culture. Those theorists who claim that socialist society is 'classless' because it lacks sharp normative differentiation have thus touched upon an important feature of this type of society. However, it would seem that this has been due less to the coercive powers of the state and party apparatus than to the impact of social mobility.

To acknowledge the degree of fluidity in the socialist system is to raise a fundamental question as to whether, or in what sense, we can regard it as being class stratified. As stated in the opening chapter, classes have generally been understood as social collectivities showing a considerable degree of continuity through time as a result of succession through the family line. In the absence of long-term social continuity and crystallization of this kind it is doubtful whether we should represent the system of inequalities in terms of a traditional class model. At any given point in time we would certainly have a ranked hierarchy of differentially rewarded positions; but if we insist in viewing class as a *process*, then we should also be obliged to consider the extent to which recruitment to these positions was determined by social inheritance. Thus, if we take a synchronic view of the present socialist reward system we can detect a distinct social boundary between the 'new class' and the rest of society. We should thus be justified in regarding it as a class system in this restricted sense. If, on the other hand, we take a diachronic view of the same system we are bound to note that this boundary is a highly permeable one in the sense that movement into the 'new class' from below is continuously taking place. Seen from this angle, the 'classlessness' thesis has greater plausibility.

Perhaps the crucial issue here is whether the openness of the socialist system can be maintained in the long run. It could be argued that the pattern of social mobility owes more to the rapid growth of white-collar positions than to political and ideological factors. The question is, if there should cease to be a substantial 'surplus' of higher white-collar jobs would the same opportunities for social promotion be made available to those born in lower strata? In other words, would members of the 'new class' be willing to accept the displacement of their own children on ideological grounds? This is likely to be a key issue in socialist society in the future. Linked to it is the problem of whether the industrial workforce will develop normative and behavioural patterns similar to those found among workers in capitalist society. These are issues which cannot at the moment be settled, although a fuller understanding of them is bound to improve our understanding of the stratification process in general. In the final chapter some of these issues are touched upon, in a highly speculative fashion, in the course of a brief summary review of 'class' problems in contemporary socialist and capitalist societies.

6 Inequality in Command and Market Systems

In the preceding pages we have touched upon a number of contrasts in the class arrangements of capitalist and socialist societies. In this concluding chapter certain other variations must also be mentioned, and in particular those having a bearing on one of the main themes running through this book: namely, the problematic relationship between inequality and political order. Both types of social system generate tensions arising from the unequal allocation of rewards, and both also contain certain 'safety valves' which tend to reduce pressure for radical institutional change. Some of these we have already examined and they are common to all types of industrial society. Others, however, appear to be related less to the forces of industrialism *per se* than to the political and economic forms which industrialism takes. For example, in comparing capitalist and socialist systems we must give due weight to the fact that one is based on a market economy and the other on a command economy. This affects not only the pattern of distribution in the two types of society but has other political and social implications. Thus, one of the features of a stratification order based primarily on the market is that the allocation of rewards is generally not in the hands of an easily identifiable and politically bounded social group. The market is a highly impersonal mechanism and the inequalities it produces derive from the free play of certain economic principles rather than from the politically motivated decisions of a dominant class. The fact that a market system is so diffuse and opaque in its mode of allocation – what Adam Smith referred to as the 'hidden hand' – has certain political consequences. This is especially so with respect to class perceptions of inequality. Max Weber suggested that political or class consciousness emerged most readily among disprivileged groups when there was a high degree of what he called 'transparency' in the reward system. That is, a condition in which members of the subordinate group are able to perceive an immediate connection between their personal situation and the overall structure of power and privilege.

The degree in which 'communal action' and possibly 'societal action', emerges from the 'mass actions' of the members of a class, is linked to general cultural conditions, especially to those of an intellectual sort. It is also linked to the extent of the contrasts that have already evolved, and is especially linked to the *transparency* of the connections between the causes and the consequences of the 'class situation'. For however different life chances may be, this fact in itself, according to all experience, by no means gives birth to 'class action' (communal action by the members of a class). The fact of being conditioned and the results of the class situation must be distinctly recognizable. For only then the contrast of life chances can be felt not as an absolutely given fact to be accepted, but as a resultant from either (1) the given distribution of property, or (2) the structure of the concrete economic order. It is only then that people may react against the class structure not only through acts of an intermittent and irrational protest, but in the form of rational association.[1] [Original italics]

In some social contexts the degree of transparency is relatively high in the sense that a dominant or exploiting class is readily identifiable by those in a subordinate status. The situation of black minorities in white-dominated societies is a clear case in point; here the social visibility of the dominant group is especially marked and the dividing line between exploiters and exploited can be represented in a fairly unambiguous way. Inequalities stemming purely from the market, however, rarely have this degree of transparency, so that perceptions and identities of a class character are less easily formed than perceptions and identities of a racial character. Runciman's work on notions of inequality in Britain has brought out clearly the inchoateness of man's view of the reward structure and his place in it. This was shown not only in the general lack of awareness of the range and extent of inequality, but also in the common tendency to explain such differences as were perceived in terms of highly fortuitous social and personal circumstances. The relatively privileged members of society were thought to be, for example, working couples without children, or men able to earn extra by overtime work, or workers employed on night shifts, and so on. There was very little awareness of a readily identifiable privileged class. This low degree of transparency in modern market-based systems stands in sharp contrast to the situation in socialist states. In the latter, the distribution of rewards is governed not so much by the 'hidden hand' of the market as by the all too visible hand of the party and the state. In so far as disprivileged groups can attribute their social and material condition to the political decisions of the 'new class', perceptions of inequality are likely to be somewhat sharper than they are in modern capitalist society. According to Geiger, 'In the USSR today social awareness of differences in material living standards is understandably extreme: there is extraordinary consciousness among the poor of the welfare of the better off, and the latter's awareness of the condition of the poor is similarly striking'.[2] Thus even though, factually, most socialist societies do not display more inequality than do capitalist ones, the consciousness of inequality is probably much sharper because of the social and political distinctiveness of the privileged. Because of the fusion of the 'new class' and the party, the social location of power and privilege in the society presents few perceptual obstacles. Under capitalism, the social location of the dominant class is less easy, as is nicely illustrated by a passage in Steinbeck's novel *The Grapes of Wrath*. The scene is where the tenant farmer, whose shack is about to be bulldozed on the instructions of the new landowners, threatens to shoot the driver of the tractor. The tractor driver protests:

'It's not me. There's nothing I can do. I'll lose my job if I don't do it. And look – suppose you kill me? They'll just hang you, but long before you're hung there'll be another guy on the tractor, and he'll bump the house down. You're not killing the right guy.'
'That's so', the tenant said. 'Who gave you orders? I'll go after him. He's the one to kill.'

'You're wrong. He got his orders from the bank. The bank told him: "Clear those people out or it's your job."'

'Well, there's a president of the bank. There's a board of directors. I'll fill up the magazine of the rifle and go into the bank.'

The driver said: 'Fellow was telling me the bank gets orders from the east. The orders were: "Make the land show profit or we'll close you up."'

'But where does it stop? Who can we shoot? I don't aim to starve to death before I kill the man that's starving me.'

'I don't know. Maybe there's nobody to shoot. Maybe the thing isn't men at all. Maybe, like you said, the property's doing it. Anyway, I told you my orders.'

In a command system, by contrast, there is much less of a problem about whom to shoot. And in this respect the conditions making for class consciousness are perhaps more favourable in present-day European socialist states than they are in capitalist states. Under capitalism, class consciousness can only properly develop under the influence of a mass political party which seeks to lay bare the intricacies of the system and its exploitative character. It is precisely because a market-based system is so diffuse in its operations, and so opaque in its political design, that the role of the radical party is so crucial to the development of political consciousness. In a command system, as in a system of exploitation based on racial differences, ideology may be rather less essential to the emergence of political awareness. That is, if there is a high degree of 'natural' transparency in the system a man does not require an elaborate conceptual apparatus to make sense of his situation in political terms.

One highly problematic issue raised here is the role of Marxist ideology in socialist states. It is not too fanciful to assume that continuous and systematic exposure to the tenets of Marxism–Leninism has encouraged a more widespread commitment to egalitarian values than is the case in capitalist society. However, by this same token, if the 'official' values of socialist society lay heavy emphasis on equality and classlessness, then any drive towards large-scale inequality is liable to produce serious tensions. At least the working class in capitalist society is not tantalized by formal claims concerning its historical destiny, innate dignity, and the like. Furthermore, it may be the case that exposure to Marxist ideology serves to heighten awareness of the social and economic forces that shape society, including socialist society. If so, this would be another factor contributing to the general sharpening of political consciousness among the subordinate class.

Set against this, however, is the fact that the party apparatus and the 'new class' control the major socializing agencies; so that like the dominant class in western society they are able to mould the popular social constructs in a manner which tends to affirm the legitimacy of the existing order. One of the key points of contrast here is that in socialist states the working class does not have access to a radical ideology which is in sharp opposition to the normative system of the dominant class. In Western capitalist societies the rise of the socialist movement brought about a distinct cleavage in the normative order by its affirmation and dissemination of an oppositional ideology. In eastern Europe, however, the dominant class itself subscribes to socialist or Marxist teachings, so that these doctrines cannot provide the normative underpinning for class conflict in quite the same clear-cut way as they have done under capitalism. Indeed, in so far as both dominant and subordinate classes subscribe to the same formal ideology, the former's ability to exercise moral, as well as coercive, control over the latter is to some extent enhanced. Normative dissensus can and, of course, does find expression through different interpretations of Marxist teachings. Thus, subordinate groups appear to stress the egalitarian elements, while writers and intellectuals are often at pains to bring out the humanistic elements; those in authority, on the other hand, are generally more inclined to emphasize those parts of the doctrine which legitimize their monopoly of political control; and so on. However, these different interpretations of the same body of doctrines do not give rise to separate, conflicting ideologies – if only because they cannot be fully articulated and developed by independent political groups. The fact that the party monopolizes control of the communications media obviously imposes a severe check on the formation of counter-ideologies. Even so, it must be pointed out that where political opposition has found expression in Eastern Europe it has always defined itself as socialist in one form or another; rarely, if ever, has the rejection of the *status quo* been aligned with support for the reintroduction of capitalism. This says much for the spread and persistence of humanistic and egalitarian strands in socialist thought, despite the fact that they have often been denied or played down in the dominant class's own interpretation of socialism.

2

Another potential source of friction in the socialist system is that associated with the opportunity structure. As pointed out in the previous chapter, mobility opportunities in eastern Europe are more favourable than those in the West. And the relative open-ness of these societies must be seen as a key factor in offsetting certain of the tensions already referred to. Favourable chances for individual advancement tend always to undermine collectivist resentments over inequality, and to encourage some degree of moral commitment to the social order. For those who are assured of a comfortable place in the reward system are usually prone to find virtue in the political and social set-up. As Azrael has written, in his discussion of the 'new Soviet men':

Raised in many instances in affluent and privileged homes, educated in the best Soviet schools, and assured of promising careers from the outset, these young people are basically satisfied with the existing system and are convinced that further 'progress' can and must be attained without departing from the fundamental tenets of Marxism–Leninism or deviating in any essential respect from doctrinally sanc-tioned goals and procedures . . . The net effect is a political outlook characterized by the intense devotion to the Soviet system and a deeply internalized and more or less militant commitment to the basic principles of social, economic and political organization that the system embodies.[3]

As we have seen, social promotion into this privileged class is also assured for a considerable minority of those not born into it. The question which remains unanswered, however, is whether the present pattern of mobility will be sustained over time. Some theorists have suggested that it will because the party would fear the creation of a self-recruiting professional and managerial class. Thus, in Feldmesser's view, 'the party must insist – in the long run – that every man be individually and continuously on trial, that status and rewards remain contingent and ephemeral. The greatest threat to the party is the development of a sense of identification or solidarity within a group – or class . . .'[4] Others, however, have argued that the tendency is for social mobility to tail off and for the class system to become much more crystallized over time. This, it is suggested, comes about largely through changes in the educational system, and in particular access to university. One observer of the Soviet system has claimed that higher education has now raised 'a barrier to entrance to the *élite* as well as providing a floor below which a member of the *élite* cannot fall'.[5] This argument is of course applied mainly to the Soviet Union since the other socialist states have not yet been faced with the same problems of social replacement. However, even in the case of the Soviet Union the evidence is by no means unambiguously in support of the 'class crystallization' view. It is undoubtedly the case that the great majority of 'new class' children continue to reproduce their parents' occupational status by way of educational achievements. But what seems to be equally true is that large numbers of workers' children are still continuing to enter higher education and professional careers. Evidence for this is furnished by a study of the student intake at the University of the Urals in the 1960s. The study showed that over half the student population were the children of skilled manual workers; at the University's Medical Institute 42 per cent were drawn from this social stratum, while in the Mining Institute at Sverdlovsk they accounted for well over 60 per cent of the undergraduate intake.[6] Thus the fact that only a minority of workers' children manage to enter higher education should not obscure the no less significant fact that they are often the preponderant social group in the student population. There is, further, little to suggest that the opportunity structure of Soviet society is now perceived as unfavourable by lower status groups, which is what we should expect to find if the class crystallization thesis were at all valid. In fact, according to Geiger, the contrary appears to be the case.

'There is considerable evidence that . . . [the] . . . image of the USSR as the land of opportunity has become ever more salient in Soviet popular culture. Indeed, no impartial investigation of Soviet daily life can fail to reveal the extent to which this belief has been accepted by the people, with reservations by the older generation, but usually quite completely and unquestioningly by the youth.'[7]

The fact that socialist societies have been more successful than capitalist societies in disseminating achievement values throughout the population may give rise to certain problems of its own. Clearly, only a minority of new entrants to the labour force are destined for higher white-collar positions, so that many others are likely to experience disappointment and frustration. This does not mean that the response to 'failure' will take on a political form, any more than it has done among the young in other achievement-oriented societies, such as the United States. But it may be the case, as Hollander has suggested, that certain types of delinquency, and similar 'irrational' protests could become more widespread.[8] However, this is all highly conjectural and it could well be very misleading to assume that status anxieties and the social punishments of 'failure' are experienced as acutely in a socialist system as they are in a capitalist system. It is quite probable that the intensity of status frustrations is partly a function of the extent of inequality in society. The greater the gap between success and failure, measured in material and social terms, the keener the sense of disappointment is liable to be. The egalitarian tendencies in socialist societies may thus ensure that unfulfilled job ambitions do not produce quite the same sense of failure that they appear to in the United States.

3

Fundamental to our discussion so far has been the distinction between a reward structure based on the market and one based on a command economy. Structured inequalities are generated in both systems, although the principal sources of inequality are significantly different. In a market-based system rewards are distributed, in the main, without direct political intervention by the dominant class; the institutional protection given to market forces, and the legitimation of market principles, gives rise to the characteristic class inequalities associated with western capitalism. The pattern of rewards and privileges is not, of course, determined solely by the operation of the market; but the market and its supporting institutions set their stamp upon the entire reward structure. In a command system, on the other hand, distribution is primarily decided on the basis of direct political agency. Under this arrangement rewards and privileges can be allocated to various social groups or strata in conformity with the aims and principles of those who occupy the seat of power. In other words, the source of inequality is primarily political, and, by this token, more readily controlled by legislative fiat.

This contrast between command and market systems has, in the view of many observers, come to stand out less clearly in recent years. This is seen partly as a result of the growth of state ownership of industry in western societies and of the increasing tendency for governments to exercise their jurisdiction in the economy. Equally, and more controversially, however, changes are also seen to be occurring in the economic systems of eastern Europe – in particular, changes designed to reduce the role of central planning in favour of a greater reliance on market factors and similar indices of economic rationality.[9] The introduction of economic reforms was a key political issue in several socialist states during the 1960s. In some cases, most notably that of Czechoslovakia, it led to bitter controversy between different interest groups concerning the future development of socialist society. It is worth examining this debate in so far as it highlights certain tensions within socialist society which are directly relevant to the subject matter of this book.

The general background to the debate was the state of the socialist economy, and in particular the mounting concern over certain of the inefficiencies associated with a highly centralized planning system. These inefficiencies have been amply documented in western analyses of Soviet-type economies. It has been suggested that under this system, planners have generally lacked adequate criteria for the allocation of resources of different sectors. The pricing mechanism has not been sufficiently sensi-

tive to factors of supply and demand, so encouraging the accumulation of unwanted goods and acute shortages of goods in heavy
demand. Given the range and multiplicity of economic decisions
that must be taken in a complex industrial system, the extreme
centralization of decision-making has almost inevitably led to
delays, waste, and bureaucratic inefficiency. In the absence of an
economically 'rational' pricing system, resource allocation tends
frequently to be based on political criteria, while managerial
authority has been subject to various forms of interference by
local party officials. Again, the system of production incentives
has been open to much abuse; managers have often succeeded
in being set artificially low production targets, thus ensuring
generous bonuses for themselves when the targets are exceeded.
Similarly, managers have been able to earn high bonuses by
manufacturing goods for which there is no demand but which
are relatively simple to produce. The literature on socialist
economies is replete with similar instances of waste and inefficiency encouraged by a highly bureaucratized planning
system.

Public acknowledgement of these problems, and proposals for
dealing with them, inspired what western observers have referred to as the 'birth of economics' in eastern Europe. Thus,
economists like Liberman in the Soviet Union, Šik in Czechoslovakia, and Behrens in East Germany, were among the leading
advocates of economic decentralization, a pricing system more
attuned to market forces, and the use of various criteria of
profitability as a measure of managerial and plant efficiency. In
the latter half of the 1960s, several east European states gave
political endorsement to certain of the reforms, although they
differed somewhat in both the extent and nature of the changes
accepted. In general, the overall strategy has been to refine and
otherwise improve central planning techniques, rather to
abandon the system in favour of 'market socialism' along the
lines already adopted by Yugoslavia.

Impetus for the reforms seems to have been stronger among
the more highly industrialized states than in the predominantly
agricultural ones. This perhaps supports the view advanced by
western economists that a command economy is relatively efficient in the early stages of economic growth, but becomes less

so when the technological and industrial base is more sophisticated and the decision-making process more complex. Thus,
Bulgaria and Rumania appear to have shown less interest in
reform than Czechoslovakia, East Germany, Hungary, and the
Soviet Union. Western observers have also tended to suggest
that reforms in the economic sphere are likely to bring about
corresponding changes in the political sphere. That is, decentralization of the economy, and the command system generally, is
seen as a prelude to the dismantling of the totalitarian power
structure and the emergence of political pluralism. The reasoning
here is that economic and political institutions in advanced industrial societies are closely interdependent, such that changes
in the former are bound to set up pressures for changes in the
latter. Developments in Czechoslovakia during the brief tenure
of the Dubček government in 1968 appear to offer some support
to this proposition; the programme for reforming the economy
quickly broadened into a more general set of demands concerning changes in the system of political control. However, it is by
no means clear that economic decentralization must inevitably
herald the onset of a pluralist political system. In Yugoslavia,
for example, the implementation of sweeping market-type
reforms has not resulted in any challenge to the party's monopoly of political control. This is not to say that attempts to
change the command economy do not throw up serious political
problems; there is in fact much evidence that proposals to
introduce economic reforms have met with sharp resistance in
all the socialist states. Conflict has been particularly noticeable
between members of the apparat and the academic economists
and social scientists who have spearheaded the drive for reform.
Apparatchiki have generally resisted the proposals partly because, if implemented, these would result in a weakening of
their own political position. An emphasis on economic rationality and profit criteria is not readily compatible with an industrial role based primarily on the exercise of political skills. At
the higher levels of authority, too, any shift from a system of
detailed planning and directives to one permitting greater autonomy at the enterprise level is likely to be interpreted, by
administrators and ministry officials, as a diminution of their
power. Similarly, not all managers would by any means welcome

decentralization and its accompanying responsibilities. As Professor Montias has pointed out in his discussion of the Czech proposals:

Enterprise directors are not all happy about the prospects for reform either. Many directors who are getting large bonuses now without great exertions are worried about the uncertainties of the future; some who banked their career on their party connections and on their understanding of the rules of the game in a command economy know they will be at a relative disadvantage when it comes to competing with men of middle-class background with experience in running a firm according to business principles.[10]

The debate over economic reform has thus, to some extent at least, also been a debate over the re-distribution of power within the ranks of the 'new class'. But certain of the changes proposed by the economists have had obvious implications for wider sections of society, and particularly for the industrial workers. The adoption of market strategies has an immediate bearing on income structure and raises crucial problems concerning inequality. Once supply and demand factors are accepted as the major determinants of reward, then men with command over skills and expertise are placed in a highly advantageous position *vis-à-vis* those lacking such attributes. Even in a command economy there is, as we have already seen, a tendency for expertise and level of reward to be fairly closely correlated; but generally speaking the range of differentials is not as wide as it would be under market conditions. Thus, professionally qualified personnel such as doctors, lawyers, academics, engineers, scientists and the like, are not as highly advantaged *vis-à-vis* the manual workers as they would be if income was determined primarily by factors of relative scarcity. At least they are not as advantaged, in relative terms, as are their Western counterparts, even allowing for the various non-pecuniary benefits they can lay claim to. In this respect, highly qualified professionals in socialist society could be said to be 'relatively deprived' in comparison with their opposite numbers in capitalist society. Consequently, if socialist states did not impose tight restrictions on the movement of personnel to the west they would probably experience a 'brain drain' of quite serious proportions. In brief, then, reforms aimed at weakening the grip of the command economy would tend to confer advantages on the skilled and qualified at the expense of the unqualified – including, of course, members of the 'new class' whose expertise was mainly of a political or ideological character. Thus, to some extent, the conflict over reforms has involved elements of a class nature in so far as it has raised the possibility of re-allocating rewards among different social groups.

Indications of the type of changes which the more radical proposals would be likely to bring about are provided by the Yugoslav experience. Yugoslavia had much earlier overhauled its economic system through a series of far-reaching reforms designed to create an institutional order based on principles of 'market socialism'. One of the most notable consequences of these reforms has been the steady erosion of the egalitarian incomes structure introduced after the revolution. The release of market forces has produced a steady drift towards wider income dispersion, favouring in particular the skilled and highly qualified occupational groups. Paul Landy, reviewing economic developments in the early 1960s, noted that, 'The most recent statistics substantiate earlier worries that "the rich will become richer and the poor will be poorer".'[11] Landy pointed out that in 1960 wages in some enterprises ranged from about 8,000 to 70,000 dinars a month; by the following year the highest salaries had increased by more than 50 per cent, while the lowest had risen by only 25 per cent. These figures refer to *individual* incomes, and it is certainly not the case that differentials of this magnitude reflect the movement of *average* earnings for different occupational groups. Nevertheless, if we examine the long-run trend of average earnings in Yugoslavia we find a clearly discernible pattern of increasing inequality.

Table 6.1 shows the average income of different skill categories as multiples of the average earnings of unskilled manual workers. Thus, in 1951 highly qualified white-collar personnel were earning only a quarter as much again as unskilled labourers; but by 1961 they were earning three and a third times as much. Highly skilled manual workers also made rapid gains over lower white-collar groups and manual labourers. These trends have continued throughout the 1960s and have given rise to considerable political anxiety. In addition to increasing income

TABLE 6.1 *Income Differentials In Yugoslavia*
(Wages of unskilled workers = 100)

	1951	1954	1957	1959	1961
White Collar					
Highly qualified ⎱	125	238	290	316	333
Qualified ⎰		155	170	186	190
Unqualified	101	123	119	132	135
Blue Collar					
Highly skilled ⎱	120	205	223	243	249
Skilled ⎰		146	149	159	160
Semi-skilled	105	118	117	125	124
Unskilled	100	100	100	100	100

Source: UN Economic Survey of Europe in 1965 Pt. II Ch. 12, Table 12.8.

inequality, the implementation of market reforms has also encouraged the spread of unemployment. One of the features of a command system which distinguishes it from a market system is the relative security of employment, especially that of manual workers. Under a command system job security tends to be relatively high partly because the indices of labour efficiency are not as sensitive as they are in a market system. Enterprises can hoard inefficient or 'surplus' labour because they are not required to operate as profit-maximizing units. Unemployment in socialist states thus tends to be of the 'concealed' variety and, as such, does not have the same social and personal implications of unemployment proper. In Yugoslavia, however, enterprises are discouraged from holding labour surplus to their immediate requirements since they are in a relatively competitive market situation not unlike that of the individual firm in a capitalist economy. As a result, unemployment has now become a serious problem. In 1952, there were 45,000 registered unemployed, or 2·6 per cent of the non-agricultural workforce; by 1963 the figure had reached 230,000 or 6·8 per cent, and it has continued to rise steadily since then.[12] The situation of the unemployed is made more critical by the relatively meagre provisions for unemployment relief. This is perhaps partly due to official reluctance to acknowledge, until quite recently, that unemployment could occur on a large scale in a socialist society. However this may be, the fact remains that the conditions attached to the payment of unemployment benefits are extremely stringent by the standards of welfare capitalism, so that only a small minority of those seeking work prove to be eligible for relief.[13]

As might be expected, unemployment does not threaten all sectors of the workforce to the same degree; it is much more likely to hit the unskilled worker than anyone else. Table 6.2 shows the occupational structure of the unemployed in 1965, and, for comparative purposes, the occupational structure of the total workforce.

TABLE 6.2 *Unemployment in Yugoslavia, by occupational skill category (1965)*

	%	(N)	Total workforce*
Unskilled manual	78·2	185,285	41%
Skilled manual	11·7	27,704	31
Lower white collar	5·6	13,255	14
Higher white collar	4·5	10,727	14
	100·0	236,971	100%

* 1960 census

Source: Vaska Duganova, 'Neki ekonomski i socijalno-politicki aspekti Zaposljavanja', *Naše Teme* (4), April 1967.

All this seems quite clearly to suggest that the erosion of a command system and the release of market forces can have a detrimental effect on the life-chances and the share of rewards of those who lack the kinds of skills which give bargaining power in the marketplace. Thus, opponents of reform elsewhere in eastern Europe have been able to point to these developments in Yugoslavia as a warning against decentralization of the economy. In particular, those whose fortunes were bound up with the *apparat* have been able to defend the *status quo* by claiming to support the interests of manual workers against the claims of the white-collar professionals for a larger slice of the national cake. Although the issue is a confused and rather complex one, it is not too simplistic to suggest that much of the impetus for economic reform did in fact come from certain groups in the white-collar intelligentsia who felt relatively disprivileged in an egalitarian system. This seems particularly to have been the case in Czechoslovakia immediately prior to the Soviet invasion in 1968. The advocates of reform in Czechoslovakia frequently and explicitly criticized the egalitarian incomes structure and argued in favour of higher rewards for qualified personnel and for those in positions of authority. Professor Ota Šik, the main architect of the new economic programme, complained that, 'greater restrictions were placed on the factors needed to ensure desired growth in the salaries of technical, educational, [and] scientific . . . personnel than on workers' wages . . . Thus, over the years, and particularly since 1959, there occurred an increasingly damaging levelling of wages, which in turn had a harmful effect on progress in science and technology.'[14] A group of economists and social scientists pointed out that in the early 1960s the total income of a university graduate working in research only caught up with the lifetime income of a worker in heavy industry when the former reached the age of 46; a doctor could not expect to overtake the worker before the age of 52, and a schoolteacher could never expect to overtake him.[15] It was on these grounds, among others, that some of the reformers pressed for 'a more clear-cut differentiation in earnings and for the more consistent realization of the anti-equalization program'.

To reach this objective, it is necessary to create, on all levels of management, favourable social, political, and economic conditions and an overall anti-equalization atmosphere . . .
Implementation of the anti-equalization program and the carrying out of a more clear-cut differentiation of wages . . . require considerable work in the areas of political education and organization, since they depend above all on personal relations and on a purposeful tightening of discipline – of both wages and workers.[16]

Given these aims, it is not altogether surprising that the opponents of reform tended to represent themselves as defenders of the working class; from their angle, socialism was being threatened at its very base by the advocates of 'capitalist economics'. The struggle between members of the apparat and the-white collar intelligentsia was to some extent symbolized in the internal party conflict between Novotny and Dubček. It is significant that in his unsuccessful attempt to retain the party leadership, Novotny and his followers turned to the industrial workers for support against the intelligentsia. It would no doubt be naïve to assume that Novotny supporters were only, or even mainly, opposed to the reforms because of the threat they posed to egalitarianism and to workers' interests generally. As already mentioned, they themselves would have been likely to lose out in the ensuing re-distribution of authority. In this respect, too, Yugoslavia furnished a disturbing precedent; there the state apparat had been seriously weakened by the reforms, a situation dramatised by the sudden downfall and public disgrace of Ranković, the head of the internal security system who was closely identified with the main opponents of reform. It is difficult to be sure how far in fact workers in Czechoslovakia were themselves opposed to the economic reforms. Strikes were reported in several of the larger towns, but there is no way of knowing how representative these actions were. It seems fair to assume, however, that workers would feel some anxiety at the possibility of unemployment and the erosion of egalitarianism. The economists and reformers themselves certainly appear to have accepted the likelihood of opposition from the workers. It was acknowledged, for example, that egalitarianism enjoyed 'broad domestic working class support', and that under the Novotny government, 'these classes have achieved their goal – a truly unique egalitarianism in the wage sector'.[17] One western observer also predicted that the reforms would bring resentment from three different social groups – 'unskilled workers seeing the wages of skilled labour going up; workers losing their jobs as uneconomic enterprises closed down or dismissed redundant labor in order to become more efficient; and finally all those members of the "New Class" displaced by the new merito-cracy'.[18]

The economists and their white-collar supporters argued that the reforms would be to the workers' benefit, since the introduc-tion of wider pay differentials would provide incentives for greater effort and efficiency; this would increase productivity and so improve living standards all round. Again, however, it would be unrealistic to ignore the fact that those groups which were most enthusiastic in their support for the reforms were the white-collar specialists who seemed most likely to gain from the erosion of egalitarianism. There is little doubt that many of the latter were greatly discontented with a reward system which seemed to them to make insufficient distinction between mental and manual work. This appears to have given rise to an under-current of hostility against the working class, who were perceived as the main beneficiaries of the existing regime. Thus some western observers have drawn attention to the 'anti-labor overtones'[19] of the intellectuals' campaign, and to the 'class bias'[20] implicit in certain of the reform proposals. These antagonisms were clearly expressed in an analysis of Czech society produced by a team of social scientists at Charles University. They were highly critical of the trend towards what they called 'vulgar egalitarianism'; this they defined as:

conservative pressure on the part of the less skilled, for whom the general objectives of revolution are over-shadowed by their traditional attitudes and limited horizons, who debase, constrain and obstruct creative work and the development of human powers, and in their failure to grasp their own dependence on scientific, technological and cultural progress, spoil the soil for a rapid advance of civilization.[21]

Adherents of this viewpoint were sufficiently powerful to engineer some of the changes they desired in the incomes structure. From 1964 onwards the salaries of qualified white-collar and administrative personnel were steadily increased relative to the wages of industrial workers. As Table 6.3 shows, the differentials were not especially great, but the general trend of incomes is illustrated clearly enough.

The arguments behind the incomes reform were not dissimilar to those underlying the functionalist theory of stratification. This theory asserts that inequality of reward is a necessary feature of any complex society, since it is a key mechanism for ensuring that talent is utilized in the most effective way. If rewards were equalized, the argument goes, there would be insufficient motivation for men to compete for the most socially important positions. Why, it is asked, would men bother to undergo long and costly training and to enter positions carrying heavy responsibilities, if the rewards held out to them were no greater than they would receive if they entered positions requiring no previous training or skill? Under conditions of equalization there would be a danger that the key positions in society would be filled by its less gifted members, while the most talented languished in equally well rewarded but less socially significant positions. As one of the Czech reformers put it, 'A

TABLE 6.3 *The trend of income differentials in Czechoslovakia* (Wages of manual workers = 100·0)

	Manual workers	*Engineering-technical personnel*	*Administrative personnel*
1961	100·0	130·8	85·7
1963	100·0	126·8	83·7
1965	100·0	135·3	86·3
1967	100·0	142·2	90·2

Source: A. Kudrna, 'Differentiation in Earnings', *Eastern European Economics*, Summer 1969.

relatively small range of dispersion in earnings ... certainly does not correspond to the *importance* and *standing* of individual professions in the national labor force and to the related claims of proficiency, theoretical preparation (education), capability and social meaning.'[22] Similar claims have been advanced in other east European states; even in Yugoslavia it was argued as recently as 1968 that 'personal income differentials are unsatisfactory from the economic point of view' because they 'do not afford adequate incentives'.[23] Claims of this kind were of course at the heart of Stalin's campaign against 'equality-mongering' in the 1930s. Paradoxically, such claims have been revived in eastern Europe not by those generally labelled 'Stalinists', but by the liberal reformers.

Objections to the first part of the functionalist claim – namely, that occupations can be objectively ranked in terms of their social importance, have already been raised in Chapter 1. The second, related claim that wide differentials are necessary to motivate men to accept the social costs of lengthy training and the shouldering of responsibilities, is much more problematic. In the first place, it is worth remembering that some degree of income differentiation has always existed in the socialist states, even though the overall range may have been narrow by western standards. Thus, even if we were to accept the functionalist case for inequality, this would not settle the all important issue of how great income differentials are required to be in order to achieve the desired ends. Given the range of differentials, both theoretical and factual, it could hardly be argued that *any* extension of income inequality, however great, was functionally required by the social system. Furthermore, to reiterate an earlier point, differences in reward are by no means confined to the field of incomes. Higher white-collar groups, even in socialist society, enjoy a variety of benefits and advantages not available to manual workers. These encompass a whole range of satisfactions and gratifications associated with creative and professional tasks, and with the favourable work environment in which these tasks tend to be carried out. Thus, even if *incomes* were to become completely equalized, the sum total of occupational rewards accruing to the white-collar intelligentsia would still be greater than that accruing to manual workers. It is therefore by no means self-evident that the absence of sharp income differentials must inevitably destroy the appeal of professional, technical, and similar higher white-collar positions. There is, after all, little evidence that the offspring of the white-collar intelligentsia are themselves anxious to avoid entering such positions in favour of employment as manual labourers. This suggests that even under conditions of relative egalitarianism rewards are sufficiently differentiated to act as a selecting mechanism, and that the advantages to be gained from the possession of qualifications are well understood by the young. If there were signs that the children of the intelligentsia were anxious to swell the ranks of the manual workers the functionalist case would seem rather more impressive. However, in the absence of such evidence we must continue to regard it with some scepticism.

In some respects the functionalist thesis could be regarded as an ideological expression of certain group or class interests. This is because it tends to be espoused most enthusiastically by those who would stand to gain by the establishment of inequalities based on claims to expertise and authority. Implicit in it, too, is the view – understandably appealing to the intelligentsia – that the possession of skills carries with it a certain moral and social superiority, quite unlike the view of man portrayed in 'vulgar egalitarianism'. The conflict over economic reforms cannot, therefore, be represented as a clash between, on the one hand, 'ideologues' concerned simply with the maintenance of their own position and privileges, and, on the other, 'pragmatists' concerned simply with 'putting the economy right'. To see the issue in these terms, as so many western economists do, obscures the point that both factions within the 'new class' tend to represent wider social groupings whose material and social situation is likely to be affected by the outcome of the debate. In this respect it must be added that the Soviet invasion of Czechoslovakia is almost bound to have an important effect on the reform programme throughout eastern Europe, and will no doubt strengthen the hand of the apparat against the liberal economists and their supporters. The invasion has dramatized the fact that the internal conflicts within socialist states between various factions and interest groups cannot be analysed within a purely national context, but must be seen against the background of Soviet hegemony throughout the European socialist bloc.

4

The contrasts touched upon above between market and command systems refer largely to differences in the structure of economic arrangements. At the same time, patterns of inequality are obviously not determined by the economic system alone, but also by factors of a directly political kind. Indeed, given the crucial importance of economic organization in industrial society, it would be unwarrantable to treat the polity and the economy as completely autonomous institutional orders. Thus, the patterns of material reward associated with a command system of the east European type cannot be accounted for without regard to the political values and aims of the party leadership. Similarly, although the market is one of the primary sources of inequality in capitalist society, it can only serve as such by virtue of the political and institutional arrangements which confer legitimacy on market principles and property rights. This suggests, then, that there is likely to be a certain degree of 'congruence' between the economic and political systems of industrialized societies – even though, theoretically, different institutional combinations and variations are quite feasible. Among the more advanced industrial societies, a market-based economy is typically found within the framework of a pluralist political system; command economies, on the other hand, typically occur in combination with a unitary or single-party political system. This relationship or congruence between the economy and political structure is of some relevance to the issue of inequality.

In modern capitalist society, for example, the combination of a market economy and political pluralism is one which makes the redistribution of advantages between social classes difficult to bring about. Legislative attempts to contain or offset the inequalities generated by the market can generally be nullified by the counter-actions of those whose material position is threatened by redistributive measures. Under a pluralist system, government is but one locus of power among many; this means that a government seeking to initiate social and economic reforms intended to benefit the subordinate class is likely to be confronted with strong opposition from multiple interest groups within the dominant class. The latter's ability to offset serious attempts to change the balance of class advantages need not make itself felt through direct political opposition (although this may often be important); more commonly, privileges can be protected through using the opportunities available for seeking other legal means for restoring the former balance. A political system which guarantees constitutional rights for groups to organize in defence of their interests is almost bound to favour the privileged at the expense of the disprivileged. The former will always have greater organizing capacities and facilities than the latter, such that the competition for rewards between different classes is never an equal contest. This is not merely because the dominant class can more easily be mobilized in defence of its interests, but also because it has access to the all-important means of social control, both coercive and normative. Given this fundamental class inequality in the social and economic order, a pluralist or democratic political structure works to the advantage of the dominant class. Only if the main political contestants were to enjoy a roughly similar economic and social status could we say that pluralist democracy was a system of genuine political equality. The fact that classic democracy of the western type accords the same civil and political rights to all social classes should not obscure the point that different groups in the stratification order are not equally endowed with the facilities for activating these rights. Thus, in the absence of socio-economic preconditions for political equality, pluralism is quite plausibly regarded as a philosophy which tends to reflect the perceptions and interests of a privileged class. If lower status groups *were* able to manipulate the legal and political system as effectively as more advantaged groups, the structure of privileges would be far more unstable than it has proved to be in most modern capitalist societies.

The combination of a command economy and a unitary or one-party system presents a different picture. Under this arrangement it is relatively easy for a government to alter the reward system in favour of previously disadvantaged groups. It is not simply the absence of a market which makes this possible, but the fact that privileged groups are not accorded the political rights and facilities for challenging or negating redistributive measures. In other words, the system of centralized power which typically accompanies a command economy is much more responsive to the aims and demands of political leaders than is a pluralist system. Of course it does not follow that the aims of political leaders are necessarily of an egalitarian kind. The case of Stalin's Russia demonstrates that it is just as possible for those in the seat of power to manipulate the reward structure in such a way as to produce more rather than less inequality. However, the political values underlying the command system are part of a broader social philosophy in which the commitment to egalitarianism occupies an important place; consequently, the powers available to leaders within this system have generally been used to combat tendencies towards inequality, not to encourage them.

What the foregoing argument suggests, perhaps, is that socialist egalitarianism is not readily compatible with a pluralist political order of the classic western type. Egalitarianism seems to require a political system in which the state is able continually to hold in check those social and occupational groups which, by virtue of their skills or education or personal attributes, might otherwise attempt to stake claims to a disproportionate share of society's rewards. The most effective way of holding such groups in check is by denying them the right to organize politically, or in other ways, to undermine social equality. This presumably is the reasoning underlying the Marxist–Leninist case for a political order based on the 'dictatorship of the proletariat'. In the absence of strict institutional controls implied in such a formula it seems unlikely – on all present evidence – that differences in social endowment would not make themselves felt in the form of pressure for differential reward. It must be emphasized here, however, that although such a process is empirically likely, it cannot be held to be inevitable; to make such a claim would be to imply that the strain towards inequality stems from something inherent in 'human nature'. And while this is a proposition which recurs persistently in the history of social thought, it is one which cannot be said to have been validated by the usual canons of scientific procedure.

Such a proposition is, in any case, implicitly rejected in the socialist model of man; here, the good society is seen as resulting from the ultimate reconciliation of social equality and political liberty. Historically, of course, socialist movements have always been concerned with the extension and consolidation of political and civil rights. The struggle for political freedoms was an integral part of a broader struggle against the social and economic subordination of the working class in nineteenth-century capitalist society. Socialist movements everywhere flourished within a social context of opposition and repression, and their efforts on behalf of the subordinate class meant that they became the standard-bearers of political liberty as a generalized ideal. A subsequent dilemma arose for socialists over the issue of whether this historical commitment to political liberty, which originated in the struggle for working-class emancipation, was to be equally binding with respect to the dominant class. That is, should socialists accord the same political rights to the economically and socially privileged as they had once demanded for the underprivileged, including the right of the former to oppose changes in the social system? The split in the European socialist movement, into Communist and Social Democratic wings, was largely the result of two different answers being given to this question. Both solutions have posed serious and unresolved problems of their own concerning the attainment of traditional socialist goals. Wherever Communist Parties have come to power they have set up a unitary political system in which the former *bourgeoisie* and their political representatives have been denied rights to oppose social change. Under these conditions, the party has been able to bring about a thorough-going transformation in the reward structure of former capitalist societies. At the same time, the party's monopoly of power has often resulted in gross abuses of constitutional rights and the use of terroristic methods of social control. Similarly, power has been used to exercise tight control over areas of social life which have little direct bearing on the maintenance of social equality. In more recent years the terroristic and coercive aspects of one-party rule have abated, but there are no signs of the party's willingness to relax its grip on the agencies of normative control, including literature and the creative arts. The fact that the humanistic ideals central to the socialist tradition have found little, if any, expression in the European socialist states high-lights an unresolved dilemma; namely, whether it is possible to establish the political conditions for egalitarianism while also guaranteeing civil rights to all citizens within a system of 'socialist legality'.

The Social Democratic solution has posed problems of a very different order. The Social Democrats have committed themselves to a political system which gives rights to the dominant class to prevent wherever possible the redistribution of class advantages. This commitment has proved to be at the expense of traditional socialist goals and principles relating to equality. As we have earlier noted, the efforts of Social Democratic governments to undermine the structure of privileges generated by the market and private property have not been impressive. This long-term stability in the reward structure of capitalist society must be understood, in large part, as a consequence of political pluralism. The experience of Social Democratic government has underlined the point that the rules of classic democracy do not in fact confer political equality on all. Political equality presupposes sufficient social and material equality to enable contending groups to utilize formal political rights in roughly the same degree. Where sharp social and material inequalities do exist, the provision of equal political rights in effect confers a major advantage on those who command the greatest resources to mobilize in defence of their interests. It is, then, against this background of chronic and persistent social inequality that we must judge the claims advanced on behalf of pluralist democracy in modern capitalist society.

Notes

CHAPTER 1

1. GERHARD LENSKI, *Power and Privilege*, New York, 1966.
2. ibid., p. 426.
3. ibid., p. 427.
4. JOHN and MARGARET REYNOLDS, 'Youth as a Class', *International Socialist Journal*, February 1968.
5. BERNARD BARBER, 'Social Stratification', *International Encyclopedia of the Social Sciences*, 1968, Vol. 15, p. 292.
6. P. M. BLAU and O. D. DUNCAN, *The American Occupational Structure*, New York, 1967, p. 7.
7. RALF DAHRENDORF, 'On the Origin of Inequality among Men', in A. Béteille (ed.), *Social Inequality*, London, 1969, p. 38.
8. LENSKI, op. cit., p. 63.
9. E. H. PHELPS BROWN, *The Economics of Labor*, Yale, 1962, p. 151.
10. J. E. MEADE, *Efficiency, Equality and the Ownership of Property*, London, 1964.
11. J. MARCHAL and B. DUCROS, *The Distribution of National Income*, London, 1968.
12. D. WEDDERBURN and C. CRAIG, 'Relative Deprivation in Work', Paper presented at the British Association for the Advancement of Science, Exeter, 1969.
13. ibid., p. 8.
14. ibid., pp. 7 and 8 (italics added).
15. H. H. GERTH and C. WRIGHT MILLS, *From Max Weber*, London, 1948, p. 187.
16. W. G. RUNCIMAN, *Relative Deprivation and Social Justice*, London, 1966, p. 38.
17. HELEN P. GOULDNER and ALVIN GOULDNER, *Modern Sociology*, London, 1963, p. 227.

18. W. G. RUNCIMAN, 'Class, Status and Power', in J. A. Jackson, (ed.) *Social Stratification*, Cambridge, 1968, p. 38.

19. T. B. BOTTOMORE, 'Social Stratification in Voluntary Organizations', in D. V. GLASS (ed.) *Social Mobility in Britain*, London, 1954, p. 380.

20. GERTH and MILLS, loc. cit., p. 188 (italics added).

21. VANCE PACKARD, *The Status Seekers*, London, 1960; THORSTEIN VEBLEN, *The Theory of the Leisure Class*, New York, 1899; C. WRIGHT MILLS, *White Collar*, New York, 1956, pp. 254–8.

22. DAVID LOCKWOOD, 'The "New Working Class"', *European Journal of Sociology*, No. 2, 1960.

23. Cf. HELEN CODERE, *Fighting with Property*, Seattle, 1950.

24. P. M. BLAU, *Exchange and Power in Social Life*, New York, 1964; GEORGE HOMANS, *Social Behaviour*, New York, 1961.

25. A. J. M. SYKES, 'Navvies: Their Social Relations', *Sociology*, May, 1969, p. 162.

26. F. M. L. THOMPSON, *English Landed Society in the Nineteenth Century*, London, 1963; ANDREW SINCLAIR, *The Last of the Best : The Aristocracy of Europe in the Twentieth Century*, London, 1969.

27. LEONARD REISSMAN, 'Social Stratification', in N. J. SMELSER, *Sociology*, New York, 1967, p. 221.

28. C. A. MOSER and J. R. HALL, 'The Social Grading of Occupations', in D. V. GLASS, (ed.) op. cit., p. 50.

29. R. BENDIX and S. M. LIPSET, (eds.) *Class, Status and Power*, Glencoe, 1953.

30. LOUIS KRIESBERG, 'The Bases of Occupational Prestige: The Case of Dentists', *American Sociological Review*, April 1962.

31. MICHAEL YOUNG and PETER WILLMOTT, 'Social Grading by Manual Workers', *British Journal of Sociology*, December 1956.

32. RALF DAHRENDORF, *Class and Class Conflict in Industrial Society*, London, 1959; JAMES BURNHAM, *The Managerial Revolution*, New York, 1941.

33. GERTH and MILLS, op. cit., p. 181. (italics added).

CHAPTER 2

1. JOHN BONHAM, *The Middle Class Vote*, London, 1954.

2. ELEANOR E. MACCOBY, RICHARD E. MATTHEWS, and ANTON S. MORTON, 'Youth and Political Change', *Public Opinion Quarterly*, (18) Spring 1954.

3. S. M. MILLER, 'Comparative Social Mobility', *Current Sociology* (9) No. 1, 1960.

4. HAROLD L. WILENSKY and HUGH EDWARDS, 'The Skidders: Ideological Adjustments of Downward Mobile Workers', *American Sociological Review* (24), April 1959.

5. S. M. LIPSET and JOAN GORDON, 'Mobility and Trade Union Membership', in REINHARD BENDIX and S. M. LIPSET, *Class, Status and Power*, Glencoe, 1953.

6. W. G. RUNCIMAN, *Relative Deprivation and Social Justice*, London, 1966.

7. WILENSKY and EDWARDS, op. cit., p. 230.

8. Cited in S. M. LIPSET and REINHARD BENDIX, *Social Mobility in Industrial Society*, Heinemann, 1959, p. 238. See also, IRVING KRAUSS, 'Sources of Educational Aspirations Among Working Class Youth', *American Sociological Review* (29), December 1964.

9. BRIAN JACKSON and DENNIS MARSDEN, *Education and the Working Class*, London, 1962.

10. W. G. RUNCIMAN, op. cit., p. 192 *passim*.

11. op. cit., p. 194 *passim*.

12. MARY D. WILSON, 'The Vocational Preferences of Secondary Modern School-children', *British Journal of Educational Psychology* (23), November 1953.

13. H. T. HIMMELWEIT, A. H. HALSEY, and A. N. OPPENHEIM, 'The Views of Adolescents on Some Aspects of the Social Class Structure', *British Journal of Sociology* (2), June 1952.

14. JULIENNE FORD, *Social Class and the Comprehensive School*, London 1969.

15. RICHARD A. CLOWARD and LLOYD E. OHLIN, *Delinquency and Opportunity*, Glencoe, 1960, pp. 106-7.

16. BRYAN WILSON, *Sects and Society*, London, 1961, pp. 113-14.

17. ELIE HALÉVY, *A History of the English People in the Nineteenth Century*, London, 1949. E. J. Hobsbawm, *Labouring Men*, London 1964 (Chapter 3). E. P. THOMPSON, *The Making of the English Working Class*, London, 1963.

18. W. PHILLIPS DAVISON, 'A Review of Sven Rydenfelt's "Communism in Sweden"', *Public Opinion Quarterly*, (18) Winter 1954/5.

19. op. cit., p. 382.

20. ROBERT BLAUNER, 'Industrialization and Labor Response: The Case of the American South', *Berkeley Publications in Society and Institutions*, Summer 1958.

21. op. cit., p. 35.

22. H. RICHARD NIEBUHR, *The Social Sources of Denominationalism*, New York, 1929.
23. CHARLES Y. GLOCK and RODNEY STARK, *Religion and Society in Tension*, Rand McNally, 1965 (Chapters 10 and 11).
24. TALCOTT PARSONS, *The Social System*, London, 1951, pp. 307–8.

CHAPTER 3

1. FREDERICK ENGELS, *The Condition of the Working Class in England in 1844*, London, 1892, p. 124.
2. JOSEPHINE KLEIN, *Samples from English Culture*, London, 1965.
3. RICHARD F. HAMILTON, 'Affluence and the Worker: The West German Case', *American Journal of Sociology*, September 1965, p. 152.
4. W. B. MILLER, 'Lower Class Culture as a Generating Milieu of Gang Delinquency', *Journal of Social Issues* (14), No. 3, 1958, p. 6.
5. H. H. HYMAN, 'The Value Systems of Different Classes', in R. BENDIX and S. M. LIPSET, *Class Status and Power*, Glencoe, 1953.
6. TALCOTT PARSONS, *The Social System*, London, 1951.
7. ROBERT K. MERTON, *Social Theory and Social Structure*, Glencoe, 1957.
8. KURT B. MAYER, *Class and Society*, New York, 1955, p. 41.
9. Cf. GABRIEL ALMOND and SIDNEY VERBA, *The Civic Culture*, Princeton, 1963.
10. ROBERT McKENZIE and ALLAN SILVER, *Angels in Marble*, London, 1968; ERIC NORDLINGER, *Working Class Tories*, London, 1967.
11. Cf. HARVEY WATERMAN, *Political Change in Contemporary France*, Columbus, 1969; GABRIEL ALMOND, *The Appeals of Communism*, Princeton, 1954, Chapter 13; NORDLINGER, op. cit., Chapter 9.
12. McKENZIE and SILVER, op. cit., p. 249.
13. DAVID LOCKWOOD, 'Sources of Variation in Working Class Images of Society', *Sociological Review*, November 1966, p. 254.
14. S. M. LIPSET, *The First New Nation*, London, 1964, pp. 110 *passim*.
15. KLEIN, op. cit.
16. RICHARD HOGGART, *The Uses of Literacy*, (Pelican edition) London, 1958, p. 92.

17. RALF DAHRENDORF, *Class and Class Conflict in Industrial Society*, London, 1959.

18. KENNETH NEWTON, *The Sociology of British Communism*, London, 1969, p. 60 (italics added).

19. ibid., p. 62.

20. HOGGART, op. cit., p. 82.

21. J. H. WESTERGAARD, 'The Withering Away of Class: A Contemporary Myth', in *Towards Socialism*, London, 1965, pp. 107–8.

22. HOGGART, op. cit., p. 92.

23. V. I. LENIN, 'What is to be Done?', *Collected Works*, Vol. 1, Part 1, Moscow, 1950.

24. H. RODMAN, 'The Lower Class Value Stretch', *Social Forces*, 1963, p. 209.

25. MARY D. WILSON, 'The Vocational Preferences of Secondary Modern School Children', *British Journal of Educational Psychology*, June and November, 1953; RICHARD M. STEPHENSON, 'Mobility Orientation and Stratification of 1,000 Ninth Graders', *American Sociological Review*, April 1957.

26. I. C. CANNON, 'Ideology and Occupational Community', *Sociology*, May 1967, p. 168.

27. Reported in *The Sunday Times*, 31 August 1969, p. 2.

28. Cf. MICHAEL YOUNG and PETER WILLMOTT, 'Social Grading by Manual Workers', *British Journal of Sociology*, December 1956; N.O.R.C., 'Jobs and Occupations: A Popular Evaluation', in BENDIX and LIPSET, op. cit.; H. T. HIMMELWEIT et al., 'The Views of Adolescents on Some Aspects of the Social Class Structure', *British Journal of Sociology*, September 1952.

29. ENGELS, op. cit., p. 122.

30. ibid., p. 123.

31. OSCAR LEWIS, *A Study of Slum Culture*, New York, 1968, p. 14.

32. PHILIP E. CONVERSE, 'The Nature of Belief Systems in Mass Publics', in D. E. APTER, *Ideology and Discontent*, Glencoe, 1964, p. 216.

33. Cited in LENIN, op. cit., p. 243.

CHAPTER 4

1. S. M. LIPSET, 'The Changing Class Structure and Contemporary European Politics', *Daedalus*, Winter 1964, p. 279.

2. CLARK KERR, *et. al.*, *Industrialism and Industrial Man*, London, 1962.

3. RALPH MILIBAND, *The State in Capitalist Society*, London, 1969, p. 98. This also contains a good discussion of the difficulties and weaknesses of Social Democratic involvement in government in the inter-war period.

4. S. M. LIPSET and R. BENDIX, *Social Mobility in Industrial Society*, Berkeley, 1959.

5. S. M. MILLER, 'Comparative Social Mobility', *Current Sociology* (9), No. 1, 1960, Table IVa.

6. KAARE SVALASTOGA, 'Social Mobility: The Western European Model', *Acta Sociologica* (9), No. 1/2, 1965.

7. O.E.C.D., *Social Objectives in Educational Planning*, Paris, 1967. Table 17, p. 187.

8. RALF DAHRENDORF, *Society and Democracy in Germany*, London, 1968, p. 108.

9. RICHARD F. TOMASSON, 'From Elitism to Egalitarianism in Swedish Education', *Sociology of Education*, Spring 1965. RICHARD SCASE, *Workers' Perceptions of Social Class in England and Sweden* (Forthcoming).

10. TOMASSON, op. cit.

11. O.E.C.D., op. cit., Table 18, p. 188.

12. ALAN LITTLE and JOHN WESTERGAARD, 'Educational Opportunity and Social Selection in England and Wales: Trends and Policy Implications', in O.E.C.D., op. cit., Table 1, p. 218.

13. JULIENNE FORD, *Social Class and The Comprehensive School*, London, 1969.

14. TOMASSON, op. cit., p. 204.

15. WILLIS DIXON, *Society, Schools and Progress in Scandinavia*, London, 1965, p. 178.

16. Cited by JOHN SAVILLE, 'Labour and Income Redistribution', Ralph Miliband and John Saville, *The Socialist Register, 1965*, London, 1965, p. 151.

17. R. M. TITMUSS, *Income Distribution and Social Change*, 1962.

18. W. FEINSTEIN, 'Income Distribution in the UK', in Jean Marchal and Bernard Ducros, *The Distribution of National Income*, 1968.

19. UNITED NATIONS, *Economic Survey of Europe in 1965*, Part II, 1966.

20. JOHN HUGHES, 'The Increase in Inequality', *New Statesman*, 8 November 1968.

21. op. cit., p. 624.

22. ROY LEWIS and ANGUS MAUDE, 'The Modern Middle Class', *The Times*, 1 October 1969.

23. C. A. R. CROSLAND, *The Future of Socialism*, London 1956, pp. 150–1.
24. See S. M. LIPSET, *The First New Nation*, London, 1964, p. 178.
25. NORVAL D. GLENN, 'Social Security and Income Redistribution', *Social Forces*, June, 1968.
26. Cited by MAURICE BRUCE, *The Coming of the Welfare State*, London, 1965, p. 13.
27. PHILLIPS CUTRIGHT, 'Income Redistribution: A Cross National Analysis', *Social Forces*, December 1967.
28. MARK ABRAMS and RICHARD ROSE, *Must Labour Lose?* London, 1960, p. 100.
29. JOHN H. GOLDTHORPE *et. al.*, *The Affluent Worker: Political Attitudes and Behaviour*, Cambridge, 1968.
30. S. M. LIPSET, 'The Changing Class Structure . . .', p. 280.
31. ROBERT MICHELS, *Political Parties*, New York, 1962.
32. HOWARD GLENNERSTER, 'Democracy and Class', in Brian Lapping and Giles Radice, *More Power to the People*, London, 1968.
33. DAVID CHILDS, *From Schumacher to Brandt: The Story of German Socialism 1945–1965*, London, 1966, p. 36.
34. MICHELS, op. cit., p. 298.
35. J. K. GALBRAITH, *The Affluent Society*, London, 1958.
36. V. L. ALLEN, *Militant Trade Unionism*, London, 1966, p. 51.
37. JOHAN GOUDSBLOM, *Dutch Society*, New York, 1967, pp. 107–8.

CHAPTER 5

1. STANISLAW OSSOWSKI, *Class Structure in the Social Consciousness*, London, 1963; G. E. GLEZERMAN, 'From Class Differentiation to Social Homogeneity', in PAUL HOLLANDER (ed.) *American and Soviet Society*, Englewood Cliffs, 1969.
2. ROBERT FELDMESSER, 'Social Classes and Political Structure', in C. E. Black (ed.) *The Transformation of Russian Society*, Harvard, 1960.
3. RAYMOND ARON, 'Social Structure and the Ruling Class', *British Journal of Sociology*, January and March 1950; 'Classe sociale, classe politique, classe dirigeante', *European Journal of Sociology*, No. 2, 1960; William Kornhauser, *The Politics of Mass Society*, London, 1959.
4. FELDMESSER, op. cit., p. 249.
5. JOHN H. GOLDTHORPE, 'Social Stratification in Industrial Society', *Sociological Review*, Monograph No. 8, 1964, p. 114.

6. T. CLIFF, *Stalinist Russia: A Marxist Analysis*, London, 1956.

7. MILOVAN DJILAS, *The New Class*, London, 1957.

8. ALEX INKELES, 'Social Stratification and the Modernization of Russia', in Black, op. cit.; J. K. GALBRAITH, *The New Industrial State*, London, 1967; CLARK KERR *et al.*, *Industrialism and Industrial Man*, Harvard, 1960. For a general critique see Goldthorpe, op. cit.

9. For documentary sources see FRANK PARKIN, 'Class Stratification in Socialist Societies', *British Journal of Sociology*, December 1969.

10. ALEX INKELES, 'Myth and Reality of Social Classes', in ALEX INKELES and KENT GEIGER, (eds.) *Soviet Society*, London, 1961.

11. ROBERT FELDMESSER, 'Towards the Classless Society?', in Inkeles and Geiger, op. cit.

12. UNITED NATIONS, *Economic Survey of Europe in 1965*, Geneva, 1966, Part II, Table 8.16.

13. ibid., Table 12.8.

14. A. SARAPATA and W. WESOLOWSKI, 'The Evaluation of Occupations by Warsaw Inhabitants', *American Journal of Sociology*, May 1961.

15. For documentary sources see FRANK PARKIN, 'Market Socialism and Class Structure: Some Aspects of Social Stratification in Yugoslavia', in S. GINER and M. SCOTFORD-MORTON, (eds.) *Social Stratification in Europe*, (forthcoming).

16. See the discussion in Chapter 1.

17. DAVID LOCKWOOD, *The Blackcoated Worker*, London, 1958.

18. NICHOLAS DE WITT, *Soviet Professional Manpower*, Washington, 1955.

19. G. V. OSIPOV, (ed.) *Industry and Labour in the USSR*, London, 1966; O. I. SKHARATAN, 'The Social Structure of the Soviet Working Class', in Hollander, op. cit.

20. VOJIN MILIĆ, 'General Trends in Social Mobility in Yugoslavia', *Acta Sociologica*, Nos. 1/2, 1965.

21. FRANK PARKIN, 'Class Stratification in Socialist Societies', op. cit.

22. ZYGMUNT BAUMAN, 'Economic Growth, Social Structure, Elite Formation', *International Social Science Journal*, No. 2, 1964, p. 213.

23. See PARKIN, loc. cit., for sources.

24. S. M. SCHWARZ, 'Education and the Working Class', *Survey*, October, 1967, p. 33.

25. DJILAS, op. cit., p. 39.
26. ZYGMUNT BAUMAN, 'The Second Generation's Socialism', (mimeo.) London, 1969, p. 12.
27. DJILAS, op. cit., p. 40.
28. HUNGARIAN CENTRAL STATISTICAL OFFICE, *Social Stratification in Hungary*, Budapest, 1967, p. 114.
29. loc. cit.
30. MILIĆ, op. cit., p. 125.
31. DJILAS, op. cit., p. 61.
32. KENT GEIGER, *The Family in Soviet Russia*, Harvard, 1968, p. 164; PARKIN, 'Market Socialism . . .', op. cit.
33. P. M. BLAU and O. D. DUNCAN, *The American Occupational Structure*, New York, 1967, pp. 436–7.

CHAPTER 6

1. H. H. GERTH and C. WRIGHT MILLS, *From Max Weber*, London, 1948, p. 184.
2. H. KENT GEIGER, *The Family in Soviet Russia*, Harvard, 1968, p. 169.
3. JEREMY R. AZRAEL, 'The Party and Society', in Allen Kassof (ed.) *Prospects for Soviet Society*, London, 1968, p. 72.
4. ROBERT A. FELDMESSER, 'Toward the Classless Society?', in ALEX INKELES and H. KENT GEIGER (eds.) *Soviet Society*, London, 1961, p. 581.
5. H. H., 'Education and Social Mobility in the USSR', *Soviet Studies*, (18) 1966–7, pp. 57–65.
6. ibid.
7. GEIGER, op. cit., p. 164.
8. 'Reflections on Soviet Juvenile Delinquency', in PAUL HOLLANDER (ed.) *American and Soviet Society*, Englewood Cliffs, 1969.
9. H. LINNEMANN et. al., 'Convergence of Economic Systems in East and West', in MORRIS BORNSTEIN and DANIEL R. FUSFELD, (eds.) *The Soviet Economy*, Homewood, Illinois, 1970.
10. Cited in GHITA IONESCU, *The Politics of the European Communist States*, London, 1967, p. 163.
11. PAUL LANDY, 'Reforms in Yugoslavia', *Problems of Communism*, November–December 1961, p. 26.
12. ROBERT G. LIVINGSTON, 'Yugoslavian Unemployment Trends', *Monthly Labor Review* (87), July 1964.

13. See the official trade union publication, *Employment and Material Position of Temporarily Unemployed Workers*, Belgrade, 1965.
14. OTA ŠIK, 'Czechoslovakia's New System of Economic Planning and Management', *Eastern European Economics*, Fall 1965, p. 22.
15. RADOVAN RICHTA *et al.*, *Civilization at the Crossroads: Social and Human Implications of the Scientific and Technological Revolution*, Prague, 1967, Vol. II, p. 39.
16. A. KUDRNA, 'Differentiation in Earnings', *Eastern European Economics*, Summer 1969, pp. 36–7.
17. VACLAV MULLER, 'The Price of Egalitarianism', *Problems of Communism*, July–August 1969, p. 48.
18. J. H. HUIZINGA, 'The End of an Illusion?', *Problems of Communism*, July–August 1969, pp. 49–50.
19. V. HOLESOVSKY, 'Czechoslovakia's Labor Pains', *East Europe*, May 1968, p. 24.
20. EDWARD TABORSKY, 'Czechoslovakia's Economic Reform' *East Europe*, April 1968, p. 25.
21. RICHTA, op. cit., p. 72.
22. KUDRNA, op. cit., p. 25 (italics added).
23. B. SEFER, 'Income Distribution in Yugoslavia', *International Labor Review*, April 1968, p. 385.

Bibliography

ABRAMS, M. and ROSE, R., *Must Labour Lose?*, London, 1960.

ALLEN, V. L., *Militant Trade Unionism*, London, 1966.

ALMOND, G. and VERBA, S., *The Civic Culture*, Princeton, 1963.

ALMOND, G., *The Appeals of Communism*, Princeton, 1954.

ARON, R., 'Classe Sociale, classe politique, classe dirigeante', *European Journal of Sociology*, No 2, 1960.

ARON, R., 'Social Structure and the Ruling Class', *British Journal of Sociology*, January and March, 1950.

AZRAEL, J. R., 'The Party and Society', in KASSOFF, A. (ed.) *Prospects for Soviet Society*, London, 1968.

BARBER, B., 'Social Stratification', in *International Encyclopedia of the Social Sciences*, 1968.

BAUMAN, Z., 'Economic Growth, Social Structure, Elite Formation', *International Social Science Journal*, No 2, 1964.

BENDIX, R. and LIPSET, S. M. (eds.) *Class, Status and Power*, Glencoe, 1953.

BLAU, P. M. and DUNCAN, O. D., *The American Occupational Structure*, New York, 1967.

BLAU, P., *Exchange and Power in Social Life*, New York, 1964.

BLAUNER, R., 'Industrialization and Labor Response: The Case of the American South', *Berkeley Publications in Society and Institutions*, Summer 1958.

BONHAM, J., *The Middle Class Vote*, London, 1954.

BOTTOMORE, T. B., 'Social Stratification in Voluntary Organizations', in GLASS, D. V. (ed.) *Social Mobility in Britain*, London, 1954.

BOTTOMORE, T. B., *Classes in Modern Society*, London, 1965.

BRUCE, M., *The Coming of the Welfare State*, London, 1965.

CANNON, I. C., 'Ideology and Occupational Community', *Sociology*, May, 1967.

CHILDS, D., *From Schumacher to Brandt: The Story of German Socialism 1945-1965*, London, 1966.

CLIFF, T., *Stalinist Russia: A Marxist Analysis*, London, 1956.

CLOWARD, R. A., and OHLIN, L. E., *Delinquency and Opportunity*, Glencoe, 1960.

CODERE, H., *Fighting With Property*, Seattle, 1950.

CONVERSE, P. E., 'The Nature of Belief Systems in Mass Publics', in APTER, D. E. (ed.) *Ideology and Discontent*, Glencoe, 1964.

CROSLAND, C. A. R., *The Future of Socialism*, London, 1956.

CUTRIGHT, P., 'Income Redistribution: A Cross-National Analysis', *Social Forces*, December 1967.

DAHRENDORF, R., *Class and Class Conflict in Industrial Society*, London, 1959.

DAHRENDORF, R., *Society and Democracy in Germany*, London, 1968.

DAHRENDORF, R., 'On the Origin of Inequality among Men', in BÉTEILLE, A. (ed.) *Social Inequality*, London, 1969.

DAVISON, W. P., 'A Review of Sven Rydenfelt's "Communism in Sweden"', *Public Opinion Quarterly*, Winter 1954-5.

DIXON, W., *Society, Schools and Progress in Scandinavia*, London, 1965.

DJILAS, M., *The New Class*, London, 1957.

ENGELS, F., *The Condition of the Working Class in England in 1844*, London, 1892.

FEINSTEIN, W., 'Income Distribution in the United Kingdom', in MARCHAL, J. and DUCROS, B. (eds.) *The Distribution of National Income*, London, 1968.

FELDMESSER, R., 'Social Classes and Political Structure', in BLACK, C. E. (ed.) *The Transformation of Russian Society*, Harvard, 1960.

FELDMESSER, R., 'Towards the Classless Society?', in INKELES, A. and GEIGER, K., *Soviet Society*, London, 1961.

FORD, J., *Social Class and the Comprehensive School*, London, 1969.

GALBRAITH, J. K., *The Affluent Society*, London, 1958.

GALBRAITH, J. K., *The New Industrial State*, London, 1967.

GEIGER, K., *The Family in Soviet Russia*, Harvard, 1968.

GERTH, H. H. and MILLS, C. W., *From Max Weber*, London, 1948.

GLENN, N. D., 'Social Security and Income Redistribution', *Social Forces*, June 1968.

GLENNERSTER, H., 'Democracy and Class', in LAPPING, B. and RADICE, G., *More Power to the People*, London, 1968.

GLEZERMAN, G. E., 'From Class Differentiation to Social Homogeneity', in HOLLANDER, P. (ed.) *American and Soviet Society*, Englewood Cliffs, 1969.

GLOCK, C. Y. and STARK, R., *Religion and Society in Tension*, Chicago, 1965.

GOLDTHORPE, J. H., 'Social Stratification in Industrial Society', *Sociological Review*, Monograph No. 8., 1964.

GOLDTHORPE, J. H., LOCKWOOD, D., BECHHOFER, F., and PLATT, J., *The Affluent Worker: Industrial Attitudes and Behaviour*, Cambridge, 1968.

GOLDTHORPE, J. H., LOCKWOOD, D. BECHHOFER, F., and PLATT, J., *The Affluent Worker: Political Attitudes and Behaviour*, Cambridge, 1968.

GOUDSBLOM, J., *Dutch Society*, New York, 1967.

GOULDNER, H. P. and GOULDNER, A., *Modern Sociology*, London, 1963.

HALÉVY, E., *A History of the English People in the Nineteenth Century*, London, 1949.

HAMILTON, R. F., *Affluence and the French Worker in the Fourth Republic*, Princeton, 1967.

HAMILTON, R. F., 'Affluence and the Worker: The West German Case', *American Journal of Sociology*, September 1965.

HOBSBAWM, E. J., *Labouring Men*, London, 1964.

HOGGART, R., *The Uses of Literacy*, London, 1958.

HOLLANDER, P., (ed.) *American and Soviet Society*, Englewood Cliffs, 1969.

HOMANS, G., *Social Behaviour*, New York, 1961.

HUNGARIAN CENTRAL STATISTICAL OFFICE, *Social Stratification in Hungary*, Budapest, 1967.

INKELES, A. and GEIGER, K. (eds.) *Soviet Society*, London, 1961.

INKELES, A., 'Social Stratification and the Modernization of Russia', in BLACK, C. E. (ed.) *The Transformation of Russian Society*, Harvard, 1960.

IONESCU, G., *The Politics of the European Communist States*, London, 1967.

JACKSON, B. and MARSDEN, D., *Education and the Working Class*, London, 1962.

KERR, C., DUNLOP, J. T., HARBISON, F. H., and MYERS, C. A., *Industrialism and Industrial Man*, London, 1962.

KLEIN, J., *Samples from English Culture*, London, 1965.

KORNHAUSER, W., *The Politics of Mass Society*, London, 1959.

KRAUSS, I., 'Sources of Educational Aspirations among Working Class Youth', *American Sociological Review*, December 1964.

KRIESBERG, L., 'The Bases of Occupational Prestige: The Case of Dentists', *American Sociological Review*, April 1962.

LENIN, V. I., 'What is to be Done?', *Collected Works*, Moscow, 1950.

LENSKI, G., *Power and Privilege*, New York, 1966.

LEWIS, O., *A Study of Slum Culture*, New York, 1968.

LINNEMANN, H., PRONK, J. P., and TINBERGEN, J., 'Convergence of Economic Systems in East and West', in BORNSTEIN, M. and FUSFELD, D. R., (eds.) *The Soviet Economy*, Homewood, Illinois, 1970.

LIPSET, S. M., 'The Changing Class Structure and Contemporary European Politics', *Daedalus*, Winter 1964.

LIPSET, S. M., *The First New Nation*, London, 1964.

LIPSET, S. M. and BENDIX, R., *Social Mobility in Industrial Society*, London, 1959.

LITTLE, A. and WESTERGAARD, J., 'Educational Opportunity and Social Selection in England and Wales: Trends and Policy Implications', in O.E.C.D., *Social Objectives in Educational Planning*, Paris, 1967.

LOCKWOOD, D., *The Blackcoated Worker*, London, 1958.

LOCKWOOD, D., 'The "New Working Class"', *European Journal of Sociology*, No. 2, 1960.

LOCKWOOD, D., 'Sources of Variation in Working Class Images of Society', *Sociological Review*, November 1966.

MACCOBY, E. E., MATTHEWS, R. E. and MORTON, A. S., 'Youth and Political Change', *Public Opinion Quarterly*, Spring 1954.

MARCHAL, J. and DUCROS, B. (eds.), *The Distribution of National Income*, London, 1968.

MARX, K., *Selected Writings in Sociology and Social Philosophy*, edited by BOTTOMORE, T. B. and RUBEL, M., London, 1956.

MARX, K., and ENGELS, F., *The German Ideology*, London, 1965.

MAYER, K. B., *Class and Society*, New York, 1955.

MEADE, J. E., *Efficiency, Equality and the Ownership of Property*, London, 1964.

MERTON, R. K., *Social Theory and Social Structure*, Glencoe, 1957.

MICHELS, R., *Political Parties*, New York, 1962.

MILIBAND, R., *The State in Capitalist Society*, London, 1969.

MILIĆ, V., 'General Trends in Social Mobility in Yugoslavia', *Acta Sociologica*, Nos. 1/2, 1965.

MILLER, S. M., 'Comparative Social Mobility', *Current Sociology*, No. 1, 1960.

MILLER, W. B., 'Lower Class Culture as a Generating Milieu of Gang Delinquency', *Journal of Social Issues*, No. 3, 1958.

MILLS, C. W., *White Collar*, New York, 1956.

Bibliography

MOSER, C. A., and HALL, J. R., 'The Social Grading of Occupations', in D. V. GLASS (ed.), *Social Mobility in Britain*, London, 1954.

NEWTON, K., *The Sociology of British Communism*, London, 1969.

NIEBUHR, H. R., *The Social Sources of Denominationalism*, New York, 1929.

NORDLINGER, E., *Working Class Tories*, London, 1967.

OSIPOV, G. V., (ed.) *Industry and Labour in the USSR*, London, 1966.

OSSOWSKI, S., *Class Structure in the Social Consciousness*, London, 1965.

PACKARD, V., *The Status Seekers*, London, 1960.

PARKIN, F., 'Class Stratification in Socialist Societies', *British Journal of Sociology*, December 1969.

PARKIN, F., 'Market Socialism and Class Structure: Some Aspects of Social Stratification in Yugoslavia', in GINER, S. and SCOTFORD-MORTON, M. (eds.), *Social Stratification in Europe*, (forthcoming).

PHELPS-BROWN, E. H., *The Economics of Labor*, New Haven, 1962.

REISSMAN, L., 'Social Stratification', in SMELSER, N. J., (ed.) *Sociology*, New York, 1967.

REYNOLDS, J. and REYNOLDS, M., 'Youth as a Class', *International Socialist Journal*, February 1968.

RODMAN, H., 'The Lower Class Value Stretch', *Social Forces*, December 1963.

RUNCIMAN, W. G., 'Class, Status and Power', in J. A. JACKSON (ed.) *Social Stratification*, Cambridge, 1968.

RUNCIMAN, W. G., *Relative Deprivation and Social Justice*, London, 1966.

SARAPATA, A. and WESOLOWSKI, W., 'The Evaluation of Occupations by Warsaw Inhabitants', *American Journal of Sociology*, May 1961.

SAVILLE, J., 'Labour and Income Redistribution', In SAVILLE, J. and MILIBAND, R., *The Socialist Register*, 1965.

SCASE, R., *Workers' Perceptions of Social Class in England and Sweden* (forthcoming).

SCHWARZ, S. M., 'Education and the Working Class', *Survey*, October 1967.

ŠIK, O., 'Czechoslovakia's New System of Economic Planning and Management', *Eastern European Economics*, Fall 1965.

SINCLAIR, A., *The Last of the Best: The Aristocracy in Europe in the Twentieth Century*, London, 1969.

SKHARATAN, O. I., 'The Social Structure of the Soviet Working Class', in HOLLANDER, P. (ed.) *American and Soviet Society*, Englewood Cliffs, 1969.

STEPHENSON, R. M., 'Mobility Orientation and Stratification of 1,000 Ninth Graders', *American Sociological Review*, April 1957.

SVALASTOGA, K., 'Social Mobility: The Western European Model', *Acta Sociologica*, Nos. 1/2, 1965.

SYKES, A. J. M., 'Navvies: Their Social Relations', *Sociology*, May 1969.

TITMUSS, R. M., *Income Distribution and Social Change*, London, 1962.

TOMASSON, R. F., 'From Elitism to Egalitarianism in Swedish Education', *Sociology of Education*, Spring 1965.

VEBLEN, T., *The Theory of the Leisure Class*, New York, 1899.

WATERMAN, H., *Political Change in Contemporary France*, Columbus, 1969.

WEDDERBURN, D. and CRAIG, C., 'Relative Deprivation in Work'. Paper presented at the British Association for the Advancement of Science, Exeter, 1969.

WESTERGAARD, J. H., 'The Withering Away of Class: A Contemporary Myth', in ANDERSON, P. and BLACKBURN, R., (eds.) *Towards Socialism*, London, 1965.

WILENSKY, H. L. and EDWARDS, H., 'The Skidders: Ideological Adjustments of Downward Mobile Workers', *American Sociological Review*, April 1959.

WILSON, B., *Sects and Society*, London, 1961.

WILSON, M. D., 'The Vocational Preferences of Secondary Modern Schoolchildren', *British Journal of Educational Psychology*, June and November 1953.

WITT DE N., *Soviet Professional Manpower*, Washington, 1955.

YOUNG, M. and WILLMOTT, P., 'Social Grading by Manual Workers', *British Journal of Sociology*, December 1956.

Index

Index

SOCIOLOGY

BLACK SKIN WHITE MASKS Frantz Fanon   50p
The experiences of a black man in a white world: A psychological
and philosophical analysis of the state of being a Negro. Fanon
portrays the Negro face to face with his race, the fact of blackness,
and the absurdity of his enslavement.

THE CHILDREN OF THE DREAM Bruno Bettelheim   75p
The dream is the kibbutz, one of the most enduring modern
attempts to create a Utopian human society. Bruno Bettelheim
examines the products of that dream and goes on to look at the
Western middle-class ideal of family.

CLASS, CODES AND CONTROL Basil Bernstein   75p
The collected papers of one of the most genuinely creative minds in
British sociology today – the development of Bernstein's theories of
the 'restricted' and 'elaborated' codes of speech and of 'open' and
'closed' rule systems. Spoken language is a process and processing
phenomenon and is the major means by which an individual
becomes self-regulating.

CONSCIOUSNESS AND SOCIETY H. Stuart Hughes   75p
The re-orientation of European social thought from 1890–1930; the
ideas and works of Freud, Croce, Bergson, Jung, Sorel, Weber,
Durkheim, Proust, Mann, Gide, Hesse, etc.

CRIME AND PERSONALITY H. J. Eysenck   60p
Are criminals born or made? Professor Eysenck examines how
heredity can determine personality differences and how 'conscience'
can act on the individual. A corrective to environmental analyses of
the cause of crime.

THE DIALECTIC OF SEX Shulamith Firestone   50p
The most articulate modern spokesman for the Radical Feminists
goes beyond Marx and Engels to find the source of all exploitative
systems in the biological/cultural relationship between the sexes –
and presents a blueprint for the first fully successful revolution in
history.

THE DRUGTAKERS Jock Young   60p
Jock Young explores in detail the nature, extent and origins of
international drug use today and shows that it is not drugs but
sub-cultures that are condemned.

EDUCATION IN EVOLUTION   John Hurt   6op
A classic of the history of education up to the Elementary
Education Act of 1870.

ETHNIC MINORITIES IN BRITAIN   Ernest Krausz   5op
Dr. Krausz examines the root causes of the wide-spread prejudice
and outright hostility that have rapidly greeted the large-scale
immigration to Britain of Jews, Irish, Poles, Cypriots, and now
West Indians and Pakistanis.

EXPLOITATION   Robin Jenkins   5op
The world power structure and the inequality of nations. This
angry outspoken book argues that the conventional approaches to
international relations, aid and development are a sham, pretending
to be scientific and objective whilst, in fact, doing no more than
defending the status quo.

THE FEMALE EUNUCH   Germaine Greer   5op
The book that caused a revolution, the central focus of the Women's
Liberation movement.

FOLK DEVILS AND MORAL PANICS
Stan Cohen   (Illustrated) 5op
Teddy Boys, Mods and Rockers, Hell's Angels, football hooligans,
Skinheads, student militants, drugtakers: these are the folk devils of
our time. A classic study of deviancy sociology.

HOMO HIERARCHICUS   Louis Dumont   9op
Ostensibly, a study of the caste system in India, Louis Dumont
sheds new light on Western notions of equality and democracy:
a classic of Anthropology.

*All these books are available at your local bookshop or newsagent; or can
be ordered direct from the publisher. Just tick the titles you want and fill
in the form below.*

Name

Address

Write to Paladin Cash Sales, PO Box 11, Falmouth, Cornwall TR10 9EN
Please enclose remittance to the value of the cover price plus 15p postage
and packing for one book plus 5p for each additional copy. Overseas
customers please send 20p for first book and 10p for each additional book.
*Granada Publishing reserve the right to show new retail prices on covers, which
may differ from those previously advertised in the text or elsewhere.*